# Navigation for Off-Road Runners

## By

## Stuart Ferguson
## &
## Keven Shevels

First published in Great Britain in 2007 by Trailguides Limited.
www.trailguides.co.uk

ISBN  978-1-905444-22-9

**Trailguides Limited**
**35 Carmel Road South**
**Darlington**
**Co Durham  DL3 8DQ**

# Contents

5

# Glossary of Terms

During the course of this book you will come across terms that you may not be familiar with. All of these terms will be explained in due course but in order to help with the flow of the book a brief glossary of them is explained below. Further detail on them will be found as you progress through the book.

Aiming-off - a navigation technique.
Catching feature - a navigation technique.
Contour features - objects on the map formed by the shape of the ground.
Fine navigation - a navigation technique.
Handrail - a navigation technique.
Harvey's - manufacturer of maps.
Line features - objects that run in a line across the map such as streams, roads etc.
Ordnance Survey - manufacturer of maps, often shortened to OS.
Point features - small, single objects that are shown on the map.
Re-entrant - a small. shallow valley.
Rough navigation - a navigation technique.
Spot height - the height above sea level of a given point.
Tick-off features - a navigation technique.

# 1. Introduction

All runners who venture outdoors run the risk of getting lost, or losing their way. It is one of the consequences of leaving the boring old tarmac and venturing towards the more exciting greenery.

Many runners, both trail and fell, stick to their same old routes confident in their ability to find their way round. The thought of using navigation can be considered akin to practising the "dark arts". But think of what routes and adventures that can open up to you by just being able to read a map correctly and use a compass.

Navigation is not difficult. All it takes is the appliance of common sense and the ability to observe. Give it a go and run a route away from the ordinary. You won't look back.

In this book we have **deliberately** used diagrams to illustrate the various points in stead of using different types of map extracts. This has been done in order to highlight the specific principles involved and not to have them obscured by the background noise that can come from the various other items shown on the map.

For a training exercise take the diagrams shown in this book and relate them to one of your local maps. Can you see similar situations and can you relate the techniques and skills shown back to that situation ?

# 2. What do we mean by Navigation

**What is navigation**
Navigation is quite simply finding your way from one point to another.
This can be as easy as finding the way from the pub to the nearest kebab
shop and as difficult as making your way across a range of mist-shrouded
mountains. All journeys, short or long, involve making your way easily
and competently from one point to another.

Many runners run off-road for training purposes. Generally they follow
routes that they know and don't venture away from them. This book is for
those runners who want to add an extra dimension to their running and
explore what awaits out there.

**Styles of navigation**
For the runner there are two particular styles of navigation and we'll
make no excuses for mentioning this several times in this book.

The different styles depend upon what you are using navigation for and
this will also effect how proficient you need to become and what particular skills you need to develop.

These two styles are
1.    Following a route, and
2.    Finding an object.


**Following a route**
Most off-road runners use navigation to follow the route of a set-course.
This will include those runners who venture off-road for fun and fitness
and will also include those runners who actively compete in trail and fell
races. In both cases the runner will be using their navigational skills to go
from the start to the finish passing all the intermediate points on the way.

**Finding an object**
Some runners use their navigational skills in a competitive sense. The
navigational ability then becomes as tested as their fitness and running
ability. Events of this type are of the orienteering and mountain marathon
variety. The aim of these events is not to find your way round a set course
but rather to find something such as a control or a checkpoint and in this
case you determine your own route and follow it.

# 3. Who Uses Navigation and Why.

All runners who venture off the beaten track, potentially, have a need for navigation skills. No matter what your walk of life, one of the prime safety skills is the ability to know where you are going. For the runner leaving the relative safety of road signs and street names, the importance of knowing where you are, where you've been and where you are going takes on a new meaning.

Many people run in the countryside just for the pleasure of being out there. Others compete in races held in the country be it fell or trail. And there is a third group who actually use their navigational skills in a competitive sense by competing in mountain marathons and orienteering events.

This book is meant for all three groups of runners, to help you master, improve and gain enjoyment out of navigation.

For runners there are two schools of navigation. The first is for those runners who just wish to have the ability to navigate round a set course and this will include those who just run for fun and those who compete. The second category is for those who navigate competitively, Obviously this takes navigation to a more advanced level than that required for just finding your way. The contents page shows each section and includes an indicator showing whether it is a Beginner, Intermediate or Advanced skill.

Below is a list reproduced from our sister publication "An introduction to Tail and Fell Running " which details the different styles of off-road event and the impact that navigation has on them.

### Types of event:
This section gives a brief summery of the nature of the different types of off-road events so that you can familiarise yourself with what to expect.

### Short Fell Races
Under six miles. With most of these events the course will consist of running to the top of a hill, fell or mountain and then running back to the finish. The route will invariably be an out and back course or a loop course with the summit at somewhere around the mid-point. There will normally only be the one major climb on these events leading up to the summit. This means that the course will probably be split 50/50 uphill and downhill. The terrain can be anything from graded track, to tussocky grass, to rocky paths, and there may be significant climbing. These

routes are sometimes marked but again there are significant numbers of them that aren't.

### Short distance Trail Races

Under thirteen miles. Runs in rural terrain normally on public rights of way such as footpaths or bridleways or on permissive rights of way (with the owners permission) over private land. A large number of events are held on Forestry Commission land. Courses are normally marked and the navigational ability required is limited to ensuring that you do not stray off-route. The climbing on these courses will be dependent upon the part of the country the event is in and may range from being flat, such as along a canal towpath, to being quite hilly. Even the hilly trail courses will not be as severe as the average fell course although there may be an overlap between tough trail courses and the mild fell race courses. The terrain involved is normally graded path or track, field paths or, normally at the worst, rough pasture. However some events do sometimes "toughen up" particular sections to make them more of a challenge.

### Medium Fell Races

Over six miles but under twelve. Not normally out and back courses but you do get the rare exception. The courses are usually some form of a loop. Often several major climbs on the route although on those races that do go up major mountains such as the Ben Nevis or Snowdon races there is just the one very big one. As a result the routes can be any proportion of up, down and level running.

The terrain can be anything from graded track, to tussocky grass, to rocky paths, and there may be significant climbing. These routes are often marked but again there are significant numbers of them that aren't.

### Middle Distance Trail Races

Over thirteen miles but under thirty miles. Runs in rural terrain as with short distance trail races. The terrain is also similar to the short distance runs. Although in certain parts of the country may include moorland paths and tracks. Due to the distances involved courses are not normally marked but they are held on public rights of way and where the course follows a particular route such as the High Peak Trail then that route's own particular way markers would provide an aid to navigation. Some events may be both TRA middle distance trail races and LDWA events with both runners and walkers partaking.

### Long Fell Races

Over twelve miles. Distances can range from twelve miles to thirty, in some cases more. Can involve long completion times. Will involve visiting several major summits with a considerable amount of climbing. Routes rarely marked and will require a degree of navigational ability. These courses normally contain a high proportion of rough moorland/ fell /mountain terrain. Should not be attempted by those runners who have no experience of travelling in this type of country.

### Ultra Distance Trail Races

Over thirty miles in distance. Some may be of considerable distance such as the Grand Union Canal Race at 145 miles. Run in rural terrain the same as short and middle distance events. Due to the distances involved these are not normally suitable for the beginner to trail running. For more information on these type of challenge events see our sister publication "Long and Ultra distance Off-Road Running".

### LDWA Events

Primarily walker's events or challenge walks. A majority of them are open to runners but not all. Although open to runners, some of these events are non-competitive and do not give prizes or issue results. However some do and it is worth checking the entry form if being on the prize list is important to you.

The events can be any distance from twenty miles upwards. They are held throughout the country so the terrain can quite literally be anything that the British countryside holds. The same applies to the amount of climbing involved, it can range from a couple of feet to a couple of thousand feet.

These events are rarely marked and require a degree of navigational competence.

Some of these events may also be registered as trail or fell races.

### Mountain Marathons

Primarily two day events although there are a number of one day and even three day events in the country. They are held in wild remote mountainous areas for teams of two. They are a two day navigation exercise with the competitors finding their way round a series of checkpoints known as controls. All food, drink and equipment required for the two days has to be carried by the competitors. These are very challenging events both physically and mentally and are wholly enjoyable as can be seen by the fact that most of the events are full before the closing date. If the thought of doing one of these monsters appeals to you then more information on equipment and training can be found in our sister publication "Mountain Marathon Preparation".

### Orienteering

A specialist form of off-road running that involves navigating your way round a laid-out course. Basically it is a competitive navigation exercise. Highly recommended for fun and enjoyment and also brushing up on your navigation skills. Orienteering courses are contained within a relatively small area by endurance running standards, so the chances of getting completely lost are minimal. There are a range of different colour-coded courses at these events to suit different fitness and navigation levels. Orienteering is outside the scope of this book but more information can be found on the British Orienteering Association's website at **www.britishorienteering.org.uk**

### Waymarking and marking of courses.

Most short trail race routes are marked in some description or another. Markers may range from the big black arrows on a yellow background as seen in many road races, to red and white or other coloured tape down to white flour arrows laid on the ground. A lot depends upon the remoteness of the course. Markers have to be transported in and the bigger and more visible the sign, the harder it is to carry. The other side is that the larger and more visible the sign, the more obtrusive it looks in the landscape. The more remoter courses will therefore have smaller signs.

Irrespective of the size of the signs it is still the runners responsibility to ensure that they follow the correct route. Running with the head down with total concentration on the running and not being aware of what is around them can lead runners to make mistakes and stray off course. Even on a marked course the runner needs to be watchful for course indicators as not all junctions may be manned, just marked.

On the subject of marking, fell races can be a totally different kettle of fish to trail runs. Fell can be unmarked, marked or a combination of the two. Due to the remoteness of the courses, fell races are normally marked with the old red and white tape. Easy to put out and easy to take back. As a generalisation it's mainly just the short fell courses that are marked, the medium and long tend not to be. However that may depend upon which part of the country you are running in, for example, races in the North East are traditionally marked, those in the Lakes not. On the race entry form or other promotional material, it will tell you whether the course is marked. But be aware that this information will normally say "partially marked". This means that the course is marked but in the case of bad weather, visibility may be reduced to a few metres and so what may be easy to follow in good weather may all of a sudden become difficult to see. If the race form does not say that the race is marked then it is safer to assume that it is not.

Long and ultra trail races and LDWA events are not normally marked. Although those events that follow long distance paths, such as the West Highlands Way race, do have the path's own waymarkers to follow. The distances in these events normally preclude the organiser marking the course and so it is left to the competitor to navigate their own way round the route.

Be aware that even on unmarked courses there may be sections that are marked and in the race instructions you will be asked to follow these markers. This is normally down to access and/or environmental issues where the organiser is required to ensure that the competitors follow a set course for a short distance. If this does occur then follow the instructions and keep to the markers. Access for future races may depend on it.

If the course is not marked then there is an obvious requirement for the ability to find your own way round the route. The ability to navigate and read a map then becomes extremely useful. Even if the course is marked, bad weather or even just bad luck in straying off-course, can result in the runner having to find their own way.

Although not normally required for shorter trail races, with long and ultra trail, fell and LDWA events it is normally assumed that the competitor has the basic ability to navigate round the course if required. On most events the checkpoint locations and normally the route descriptions are known long before the event. This can allow the competitor to recce the route before race day and iron out any possible navigation difficulties. Something that is always recommended.

Even when just on a training or recreational run, the ability to navigate can open up a whole new dimension to your running.

# Checkpoints and controls

On most events, the target that you are normally aiming for is a checkpoint or control. Dependant on the type and aim of the event these are not necessarily the same thing. So what are they and what are the differences.

### Checkpoints

Checkpoints are normally on events where the testing of navigational skills is not the prime activity of the event. These are races either trail, fell or LDWA where the aim is to run round a set course. Checkpoints are placed around the route to ensure that the runner adheres to the course. The runner being required to visit each checkpoint in turn. The checkpoints also act as safety nets, they ensure that the competitors have safely reached and passed through a particular section of a race.

There is no particular physical aspect of a checkpoint. Many of them consist just of a marshal standing on top of a hill or at a path junction. Often there is more than one marshal to keep each other company during the long lonely moments. In long distance events some checkpoints may also double as a feed station. Occasionally a checkpoint may be unmanned, in which case there may be something such as a bucket for the runner to drop a tag into to prove that they have passed or a clipper so that the runner can self-clip their number or tally card.

Checkpoints are normally quite visible. There are no attempts to hide them because the aim of the event is not to find the checkpoint but rather

Typical event checkpoint doubling-up as a feed station. Fairly easy to spot.

to pass through it on the way round the course. Quite often if the marshals see that the runner may miss or go past the checkpoint then they will attract the runners attention to keep them on track. The marshals are also quite willing to point out the way and give navigational advice.

## Controls

Controls are on events where the principal activity of the event is to test the competitor's navigational skills. The aim is for the competitor to make their way from control to control by whichever route they consider to be the fastest and most effective. There is no set route for the competitor to follow, route choice is dependent upon the competitor's own decisions.

Controls almost always include an orienteering kite and either a control punch or electronic dibber. On some events the control is manned, on other they are not. Some events have a mixture of manned and unmanned controls.

Controls are not obviously visible. The aim of the event is to navigate to and find the control. While not deliberately hidden, they are placed in positions that are not immediately visible, for example on the opposite side of a boulder from the obvious approach direction. When manned, the marshals at a control will give no navigational assistance to the competitor. They normally stay as unobtrusive as possible to avoid attracting attention and inadvertently guiding the competitors in to the control. In the Saunders Lakeland Mountain Marathon for example, the control marshals spend the whole weekend out at the controls, camping overnight. Even their tents are green in order to blend into the landscape and be as unnotice-

able as possible.

Event control on a wild wind-swept moor. While not hidden, the skill is in locating them.

16

# 4. Access.

In the previous section we discussed who uses navigation. As a competitor on an event, access to the event area either on public rights of way or more open access will have been arranged by the event organiser. However, for the recreational runner or the runner just out training a fundamental part of navigation is knowing where you can, quite legitimately, go. This section looks at rights of way and access in the countryside.

## England and Wales

### Rights of Way
Strictly speaking a right of way is not actually a path. Instead it is a right that is possessed by the public to pass and re-pass along a linear route.
There are a number of different categories of rights of way. These are classified as follows.

### Footpath.
Open to pedestrian traffic only. Footpath signs and waymarkers use a yellow arrow. Shown on maps by
OS 1:50,000 - short-dashed pink line.
OS 1:25,000 - short-dashed green line.
Harvey's     - solid green dotted line (if a path exists on the ground the dotted line is accompanied by a dashed black line).

### Bridleway.
Open to pedestrians, cyclists and horse riders. Signed and waymarked with a blue arrow. Shown on maps by
OS 1:50,000 - long-dashed pink line.
OS 1:25,000 - long-dashed green line.
Harvey's     - line of green circles (if a path exists on the ground the line of circles is accompanied by a dashed black line).

### Byway Open to All Traffic ( BOAT ).
Open to pedestrians, cyclists, horse riders and motor vehicles. Signed and waymarked with a red arrow. Shown on maps by
OS 1:50,000 - a pink short dash, followed by a cross.
OS 1:25,000 - a series of green crosses.

**Restricted Byway**
Open to pedestrians, cyclists, horse riders and non-motorised vehicles.
Shown on maps by
OS 1:50,000 - a pink long dash followed by a short dash.
OS 1:25,000 - a green long dash with a short perpendicular line coming
from the centre.

**Unclassified Road**
Open to pedestrians, cyclists, horse riders and motorised traffic. Shown on
maps by
OS 1:50,000 - pink dots.
OS 1:25,000 - green dots.

**Permissive Footpath.**
A path where the landowner has allowed public access on foot only. Shown
on maps as
OS 1:50,000 - not shown.
OS 1:25,000 - short-dashed orange line.
Harvey's      - line of blue circles.

**Permissive Bridleway.**
A path where the landowner has allowed public access on foot, cycle or
horse. Shown on maps as
OS 1:50,000 - not shown.
OS 1:25,000 - long-dashed orange line.


Don't be fooled by what a right of way looks like. Quite often there is no
visible trace of a path or track on the ground. Most paths are maintained by
people using them, if they are seldom used then they get overgrown and
indistinct which can make them difficult to follow.


The picture on the right shows a
public bridleway which is legally
accessible to pedestrian traffic,
horse-riders and cyclists. It is hardly
used and virtually non-existent on
the ground. There is no visible trace
of a path going across the field.

In contrast the picture on the left is a public footpath. By co-incidence it runs along a well-made farm track. Despite the prominent good surface, this track is only legally accessible to foot traffic. Horse-riders, cyclists and other forms of user are not allowed.

## Access Land

In 2005 the final parts of the Countryside and Rights of Way Act 2000 (CRoW) finally allowed walkers and runners to legally roam freely on designated access land without the need to keep to official paths and bridleways. The new edition of the Ordnance Survey Explorer map shows this land marked with an orange coloured border and a light yellow coloured background. At many of the access points to this land, the stiles and gates carry a disk with the new access land way-marking symbol of a brown stick man in a brown circle. At certain spots there will also be signs showing your rights and obligations under the new act and also whether there are any restrictions in force. The map shows these information points as A.

Not that all land is access land. For obvious reasons the right to roam does not apply to cultivated land. The Countryside and Rights of Way Act 2000 (CRoW), applies only to mapped areas of uncultivated, open countryside namely mountain, moor, heath, down and registered common land.

The right to roam can be restricted by farmers and land owners for up to 28 days each year, Normally this would be tied in with the lambing or nesting seasons. For more information about access and up to date information on restrictions see,
**www.countrysideaccess.gov.uk**.

## Scotland

The Scots, being an enlightened people, have very enlightened access rights, The Scottish outdoor access code places the emphasis on responsible use rather than where you can or cannot go. Everybody has access rights in law under The Land Reform (Scotland) Act 2003 over most land provided that this access is exercised responsibly. There are obviously some exceptions such as private gardens, fields, quarries, railways etc. For more details on the access code see
**www.outdooraccess-scotland.com**

# 5. Tools.

Navigation as with every trade, has it's own particular tools of the job. In this section we will examine each of the main tools and see why and how they are used. To assist you decide the importance and relevance we have categorised each of the tools into:
Essential – do not venture outdoors without them.
Support – nice to have.

The matrix below is in relation to navigation only and does not cover the likes of safety, refer to the specific books within our series for more details on safety equipment.

| Tool | Essential | Support |
|---|---|---|
| Eyes | Yes | |
| Map | Yes | |
| Traditional Compass | Yes | |
| Electronic Compass | | Yes |
| Altimeter | | Yes |
| GPS | | Yes |
| Red pen. | | Yes |
| Roamer. | | Yes |
| Pacing scale. | | Yes |
| Pedometer | | Yes |
| Thumb | | Yes |
| Map Measurers | | Yes |
| Watch. | | Yes |
| Mapping Software | | Yes |

We will now look at each of these in turn.

# Eyes

These are very underestimated, the eyes being the most important tool to the navigator. Observation is the key to successful navigation. Keen eyes and an alert mind are essential in extracting detail from the map and looking for clues in the landscape to marry-up to the map.

Obviously eyes enable you to look at the map but don't just look at the map, examine it in detail, make sure that you extract all the information that you need both to plan and follow your route. If necessary use the magnifier on your compass to help see the small detail.

The eyes also tell you the nature of the terrain in front of you. They will enable you to compare what is physically there to what is on the map. Both eyes and mind need to be alert in order to spot all the little features that tell you that you are on course or, even more importantly, tell you that you are going off-course.

You will also need to look at the ground in front in order to make a good route decision. Using observation may enable you to avoid poor running areas such as marshes, rocks and heather, while at the same time identify good running areas such as level ground and sheep trods.

Careful observation can also help you predict the weather, seeing whether rain clouds are being blown in, whether fog is descending, etc. All the factors can have an influence on your route decisions and possibly your safety.

The navigator who is not observant is only operating with half their ability.

The eyes compare the map to the ground in front of you and show you where to go. Following a well-defined track like this is relatively easy but you still need to keep your eyes open to identify features that will show how far along the track you are. One of the keys to successful navigation is to be constantly aware of your position.

Use the eyes to look ahead and see where you are going and compare the landscape against the map. This helps you to keep moving and reduce the instances of time-wasting while standing still looking at the map. In this instance looking down the slope will identify the fence on the other side of the valley which will be followed as a handrail.

When running across agricultural land the line of the path may not be so obvious. This may be down to infrequent use, congestion due to large numbers of fences, hedges and/or walls or even due to the field being ploughed. In lowland navigation observation plays a greater part than you would first think. The first tip is to always try and identify any waymarkers that may exist. The second tip is to try and see the exit point. For example, look for the stile on the other side of the field, the path will almost certainly be a straight line from you to it.

# Maps

A map is a picture of a landscape. It represents all the information about an area of land on a flat piece of paper that can be read and used to guide you. A map gives you the ability to navigate to places that you are unable to see ahead of you.

A map is the essential piece of navigation equipment. Without one finding the way is extremely difficult. Because of it's importance a full section has been devoted to maps and map reading. See Section 6 Map Reading.

# Compass

At it's most basic the compass is nothing more than a magnetised bar of metal that is suspended in the earth's magnetic field. The importance of this to the navigator is that it can be relied on to constantly point to one fixed point of reference, the magnetic north pole. From that all other directions can be calculated.

In essence navigation is a joint exercise between the eyes, the map and the compass. In good visibility with well-defined terrain it is possible to navigate using just map reading. However when the landscape becomes featureless and/or the visibility is bad the usefulness of the map becomes more limited. In these cases the importance of the compass moves up substantially and is indispensable when considering safe navigation.

The techniques of using a compass are looked at in Section 7 Fundamental Skills.

### Selecting a compass.
The compass you choose is a very crucial part of your toolkit. There are many varieties on the market.

1.  Toy ones that come out of Christmas crackers. These are not durable enough and have virtually no features.
2.  Electronic ones such as watches. These are not very accurate or feature rich but may have an altimeter incorporated.
3.  Thumb ones specifically developed for orienteering. No base plates.
4.  GPS – see specific section.
5.  The protractor style. This is the most common type used by most people.

It is recommended to purchase a protractor compass for accuracy, durability and features. The compass should be compact, robust, light in weight and capable of being easily used in bad weather conditions. The capsule holding the needle should be liquid filled to enable the needle to settle down quickly when the compass is moved or rotated. In addition the rim of the housing should be marked off in 360 degrees which will be used to read the angle of bearing. There a number of companies that supplies such items. The main ones being:

| Suunto | Silva | Recta |
|--------|-------|-------|

## Parts of a Standard Protractor Compass

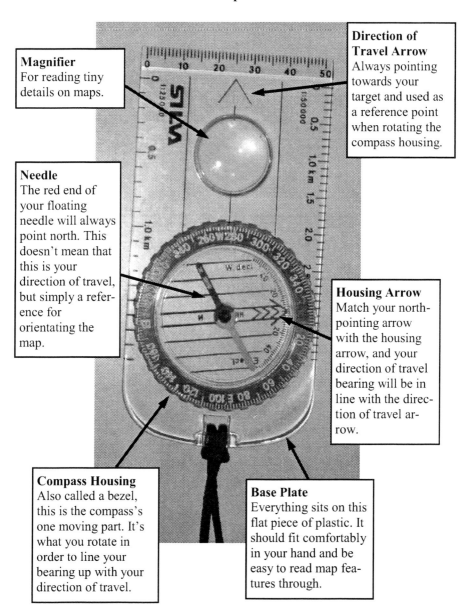

**Magnifier**
For reading tiny details on maps.

**Direction of Travel Arrow**
Always pointing towards your target and used as a reference point when rotating the compass housing.

**Needle**
The red end of your floating needle will always point north. This doesn't mean that this is your direction of travel, but simply a reference for orientating the map.

**Housing Arrow**
Match your north-pointing arrow with the housing arrow, and your direction of travel bearing will be in line with the direction of travel arrow.

**Compass Housing**
Also called a bezel, this is the compass's one moving part. It's what you rotate in order to line your bearing up with your direction of travel.

**Base Plate**
Everything sits on this flat piece of plastic. It should fit comfortably in your hand and be easy to read map features through.

When first looking at protractor compasses ones you will notice short base plate and large base plate models. Select a large base plate compass as this increases accuracy especially over the longer legs.

Check the edge of the compass, it should have measurements marked along the base plate graded to relevant map scales, normally 1:25,000 and 1:50,000.

Open up and try the turn of the unit, some have different feelings to their movement and try it in your hand as if you are carrying it.

Does the unit have a nice feel, is it within budget, and has all features you require – purchase.

## Problems with compasses

The main problem with compasses is that of robustness. They can be fairly fragile objects and easily damaged. A number of competitors do carry a spare just in case the worst happens.

Another common problem is not so much with the compass but rather the human memory and that is with the compass being a relatively small piece of equipment, it is easy to forget. Always double-check that it is packed before the event.

## Electronic compasses

There are many such devices on the market especially ones built into watches. These are best used for very rough navigation only and should not be relied on for fine navigation. Always carry a standard compass. **Beware this is an aid only and like all electronic devices can be affected by weather conditions and the health of the power source – the battery.**

# Altimeter.

Although you can buy stand-alone altimeters, for the runner it is the many watches which come with altimeters in as standard that are of particular interest. Altimeters identify the spot height above sea level and work by sensing changes in air pressure when ascending or descending.

These devices are useful when trying to find a feature at a certain height or when contouring around a feature. To ensure the accuracy of the altimeter it needs to be regularly re-calibrated from known spot heights, for example, trig points.

Altimeters are a useful aid for the competitor especially for contouring and finding that checkpoint on a spot-height "re-entrant at 800 metres". Although altimeters are allowed in most events one event, the Capricorn, has disallowed them. However be aware that some events, for example the OMM, use maps with no height narrative on the index contour which can make altimeters less useful.

Altimeters use barometric pressure sensing, this also can be a useful aid to roughly predicting the weather by just watching the pressure move. If the pressure goes lower then the prediction will be bad weather coming in, if the pressure goes higher then the weather will be improving.

**Beware this is an aid only and like all electronic devices can be affected by weather conditions and the health of the power source – the battery.**

If using an altimeter take every opportunity to re-calibrate when you come across an identifiable height feature, in this case the cairn. Identify the height of the cairn from the map and ensure that the altimeter agrees with it.

# GPS

Global Positioning System is a satellite based navigation system utilising a network of twenty seven satellites in orbit around the earth. The data from these satellites when captured by a GPS receiver helps to determine any location on the planet to an accuracy of between ten to twenty metres.

There are two types of GPS currently on the market:
1.      Ones that give live position fixing, and
2.      Ones that give a retrospective training log.
The second option , which includes models such as the Garmin Forerunner, will not tell you where you are but will tell you where you have been. Not very helpful for navigation. Ensure that your GPS does actually do what you think it does.

GPS receiver units are getting smaller and smaller with added features and improved battery life. Utilising mapping software on your PC you can download routes to follow co-ordinates when out in the field, you can see real time positioning, speed over ground, height, compass functions, barometer to help predict weather. If you have been out for a run when back at home you can upload your route onto your PC, check distance run, height gain and also store for future use.

Even if you use a GPS you still need to be able to use a map and compass competently as GPS units can fail, batteries pack up and more importantly try to find a checkpoint when the fog is down and your GPS is at thirty metre accuracy. **Beware this is an aid only and as all electronic devices can be affected by weather conditions and heath of the power source – the battery.**

Going to the ins and outs of how to operate a GPS is outside the scope of this book. If you have one refer to the unit's instruction book. However, if you do use one then you do need to be aware of some of their limitations.

1 Losing the signals.
The receiver depends on a signal beamed down from a satellite system that surrounds the globe. It is possible to lose the signal if the receiver is not in the line of sight with at least three of the satellites. This can happen in a steep gorge or heavy woodlands, for example.

2. Aiming for the nearest waypoint.
When you input a route into a GPS receiver you input a number of grid

reference targets or waypoints. Making your way round these waypoints forms a route. However some GPS receivers may aim for the nearest waypoint, not necessarily the next in numeric sequence. In certain circumstances this may present a dangerous situation if, for example, interspersed between the two waypoints was a cliff.

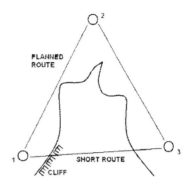

**Can you use a GPS on an event.**
This is a bit of a grey area. In those events where the primary aim of the event is to test your navigational ability such as mountain marathons or other long navigational events then the answer is a definite no. In other events where the aim is to run round a set course then the answer is maybe. There is no definite ruling but is generally accepted that if the rules of the competition do not specifically forbid the use of a GPS then it is acceptable to use one.

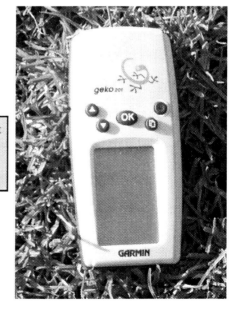

One of the many different makes of GPS on the market.

**Global Positioning System (GPS)**, is currently the only fully functional Global Navigation Satellite System (GNSS).

Developed by the United States Department of Defence, it is officially named **NAVSTAR GPS** (**NAV**igation **S**atellite **T**iming **A**nd **R**anging **G**lobal **P**ositioning **S**ystem). Over twenty four satellites are in Orbit. The satellite constellation is managed by the US Air Force. This GPS is free for civilian use.

There is one other active system **GLONASS** (**GLO**bal **NAV**igation Sataelliet **S**ystem) a Russian developed system with around twelve satellites in orbit.

There are currently a number of other new systems in the pipeline, notably the EU is developing **GALILEO** (**G**alileo **P**ositioning **S**ystem) which is planned to be operational in 2010.

## Red pen

With any navigation there will be a need to mark the map with the location of the checkpoints/controls. With competitive navigation, there may be a need to mark other things such as out-of-bounds areas, etc. Any colour pen could be used for marking-out these items. However, most people do tend to use a red pen. Red is a colour that is not naturally occurring on the map. Therefore anything marked in red will stand-out, away from the background information of the map.

Some runners tend to carry a small piece of fine sandpaper to rough-up laminated paper when wet so that the ink from the pen latches on to the wet map.

## Roamer

A clever little device that assists in accurately transferring the third figure of a three figure grid reference onto a map. It breaks the one kilometre measure on the northing and easting down into the 1/10th required for the third number. Can be obtained in different sizes for different map scales although most roamers will accommodate several scales.

## Pacing scale

A pacing scale is a gauge of distance covered in relation to the number of steps taken. This topic is covered in more detail in Section 8 Advanced Skills - Estimating Distance Using Pacing.

## Pedometer

Another tool which can be used to count single paces rather than doing it in your head. This is a small unit that fits to a belt or similar place and registers the vibration from your foot hitting the ground as it moves up your body and trips a sensor in the unit.

# Thumb

Never mind the thumb being useful for 'thumbing the map', see Section 7 Fundamental Skills, but it is also useful for another navigation technique. Check the length of your thumb from tip to knuckle and work out it's scale relative to the distance on a map. During 'very' rough navigation you can quickly work out distance by the number of thumb lengths along the line of travel. For example, if your thumb length is equivalent to one mile, so then three thumb lengths equates to three miles. Use correlation against time and this gives you another pointer as to when you will arrive at your destination.

# Map measurers

A map measurer is a little gadget rather like a pen that can be run over a route on the map and which will calculate the distance. The measurer can be electronic or mechanical which operates a wheel at it's base. Typically it will be able to work with eight different map scales and will give the result in miles and/or kilometres. Normally the map scales capable of being used are:

1:750000
1:500000
1:400000
1:200000
1:100000
1:500000
1:250000
1:150000

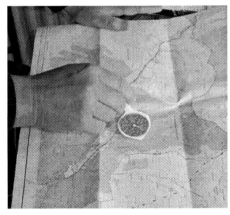

In practical terms these measurers are not much use out in the field to measure distance but can be useful in gauging distance pre or post run at home.

# Watch

Most runners carry a watch while out running. In addition to the normal reasons of timing your runs and races, you can use time to correlate against distance and judge how far you have travelled. For more detail see Section 8 Estimating distance using time.

# Mapping software

There are currently two types of mapping software on the market:

1. Electronic Maps. Gone are the days of buying maps from a shop, it is now possible to purchase electronic map software to load onto your PC. You can plan and print out routes of your choice and then print out onto paper including waterproof types. The routes can also then be stored and then downloaded to your GPS. There are a number of different programs available on the market including some with added features such as aerial photography.

2. Educational or Training programs. These typically will navigate you through a series of tutorials on navigation, in differing locations and in differing weather conditions. They are fun and help keep your hand in from the comfort of your home.

# 6. Map Reading.

A map is a pictorial representation of the land. It uses pictures and symbols to represent the nature and features of the landscape. Using a map allows you to see into the distance to what, physically, can't be seen with your own eyes.

Most maps contain hundreds of thousands of bits of information about the ground. However not all of these are of relevance to the navigator. In fact, because of the demands of different interest groups most maps end up being a compromise over the amount and type of information being shown.

Whilst it is important for the navigator to be able to use the maximum amount of data shown by the map, it is also vital to know what information is not shown by the map. For example, maps do not give very much information about the nature of the terrain and how easy or difficult it is to walk or run over. There are no symbols for waist-deep heather or peat bogs.

In this section we will look at maps and the skill of map reading, interpreting the map so that you understand what it is telling you.

1.      Types of map.
2.      Anatomy of a map.
3.      Map scale.
4.      Grid lines.
5.      Contour lines.
6.      Concave and convex slopes.
7.      Line features.
8.      Contour features.
9.      Point features.
10.     Symbols on maps.
11.     Boundaries.
12.     Other items shown on maps.
13.     Magnetic variation.
14.     The importance of trig points.
15.     The problems with maps.

# Types of Map.

In the UK there are four types of map generally used for navigation.
These are

1. Ordnance survey   1: 50,000
2. Ordnance survey   1: 25,000
3. Harvey's          1: 40,000
4. Specialist orienteering maps, can be any scale but usually 1:5,000, 1:7,500 or 1: 10,000

The main difference between these maps is the scale at which they are plotted and the corresponding detail that each size allows to be printed on the map.

Both the Ordnance Survey (OS) maps, 1:50,000 and 1:25,000 are general purpose maps and are not aimed specifically at the outdoor market. They contain lots of information that is not necessary for the navigator, for example, county and parish boundaries. By the same token they also do not contain certain information that would be extremely useful to the outdoor person such as vegetation type and ground surface. Both of these map series cover the whole of the UK.

Ordnance Survey maps are the most widely used maps for outdoor pursuits in the UK, in particular the 1:25000 series.

Note that there is not a constant colour coding or range of symbols between the two OS maps series. For example, public rights of way are shown as red on the 1:50000 maps and shown as green on the 1:25,000.

Harvey's maps are specialist maps produced with the outdoor enthusiast in mind. As such non-relevant information is generally excluded and there is more detail on other aspects such as type of vegetation and ground surface than on a corresponding OS map. Harvey's maps do not cover the whole of the UK instead they focus in on the main outdoor activity areas.

Harvey's maps are popular with the outdoor fraternity because of their specialisation. In those events where a map is provided to competitors, such as mountain marathons, then it is normally a Harvey's map.

Note the symbolism and colour coding between OS maps and Harvey's maps are different.

Orienteering maps are specifically produced by orienteering clubs for their own events. They are highly detailed and often contain more information on features, vegetation and ground surface than you would find on either OS or Harvey's maps. They are only produced for event areas where the orienteering clubs have permission to hold events. They are not generally available to the public. It doesn't happen often but occasionally a non-orienteering event will hold an event using an orienteering map.

Because of their size, maps come conveniently folded to make them easy to carry. To protect them they have a cardboard cover. They are normally printed on tough but non-waterproof paper however laminated versions of most maps are available.

Maps supplied at events are normally given out just as a sheet with no protective cover although quite often they are printed on some form of waterproof paper.

From left to right. OS 1:50,000, Harvey's 1:40,000, OS 1:25,000, Harvey's 1:40,000 sheet given out at a mountain marathon, and, bottom, specialist orienteering map from a permanent course.

# Anatomy of a Map

When you unfold your map your will typically have a 93 by 124 cm size sheet. The majority of the sheet is taken up by the map content whether it is single or double sided but there is also some very useful, often overlooked information also included. Among other things this includes the table of symbols used to represent the information contained within the map.

Take for example the OS 1:25000 Explorer Series front sheet. Normally on the right hand side of the map there is a box or tool bar containing the following information. If the map is double-sided then this is usually only shown on the one side.

| Customer Information | Giving edition and date when the map was last revised. |
|---|---|
| Communications | Roads and Paths |
| | Railways |
| | Public Rights of Way |
| | Other Public access |
| General Information | Access land |
| | Boundaries |
| | General Features |
| | Archaeological and Historic Information |
| | Vegetation |
| | Heights and Natural Features |
| | The National Grid System |
| | North Points |
| Selected Tourist and Leisure Information | General tourist information. |

Running along the bottom of the map is a small table showing the scale of the map which also shows sample measurements in kilometres and miles. There is also a conversion table giving the conversion factors to change kilometres to miles and metres to feet and vice versa. This is shown on both sides of the map if double-sided.

# Map Scale

The scale of a map is always printed on the map cover. This is expressed as the ratio between a unit of length on the map and the equivalent distance on the ground. Therefore a scale of 1:25,000 means that one centimetre on the map is the equivalent of 25,000 centimetres on the ground. 25,000 centimetres being 250 metres. In the same way 1:50,000 means that 1 centimetre on the map is equal to 50,000 centimetres (500 metres) on the ground.

## Map scale differences.

### 1:25000
1 km = 4 cm on map.
There is a high level of detail contained on these maps, in particular field boundaries such as walls and fences. This allows you to navigate to a higher degree of accuracy. On the downside there is at sometimes too much detail, this can be sometimes be confusing and can occasionally obscure out some important features such as paths.

**1:40000** 1 km = 2.5 cm on map.
This gives about the correct amount of detail for good fine navigation The colouring allows good land form aspect. The use of 15m contours as opposed to 10m is very difficult to use.

Probably the optimum size. It is capable of providing sufficient detail to allow fine navigation while covering a relatively large area on the one map. However the use of 15 metre contour intervals can be difficult to get used to especially for those more used to the OS 10 metre intervals.

### 1:50000
1 km = 2 cm on map.
This map is good for rough navigation. The lack of detail and the omission of some features make this map difficult to use for fine navigation, however, the smaller scale can mean that fewer maps are needed to cover a large area.

# Grid Lines.

The first thing you should notice on the map are a series of straight vertical and horizontal lines that run across the face of the map. These are the grid lines that correspond to the national grid and are used to pinpoint positions on the map.

Understanding and using grid lines and grid numbers is explained in more detail in Section 7. Fundamental Skills.

# Contour Lines

The face of the map has a number of brown lines flowing across it. These are known as contour lines and are used to represent the height and steepness of the ground and very importantly if read correctly they will also show a profile of the landscape.

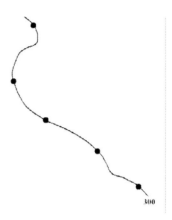

The contour lines link spots of equal height, so, if for example, you have a contour line as right, every spot along that line is the same height of 300 metres above sea level.

The contour lines occur at regular intervals. With OS maps this interval is 10 metres, with Harvey's maps the intervals are 15 metres. This interval is the vertical height between each contour line.

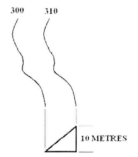

To travel from one contour line to the next means that you vertically climb 10 metres.

With having the contour lines spaced at equal height distances apart this means that the steepness of the land can be easily read by using the space in-between each line as a measure. If the lines are closely grouped together then the slope of the ground is steeper than when they are more widely spaced apart.

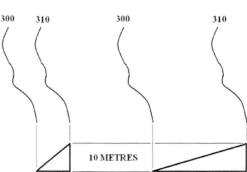

This explains why maps of the more mountainous areas look more congested than those of low-lying areas. The ground is steeper so therefore the contour lines are more closely grouped together and there is more variation in height, i.e. more ups and downs and therefore more contour lines.

Having a mass of contour lines running across the map can make it difficult to read the individual lines. To make reading easy, every fifth line is shown in bold as a thicker line. With OS maps having the contours spaced 10 metres apart this would make the 50 metre interval being heavily printed and with Harvey's using a 15 metre interval, this would give the thick line a 75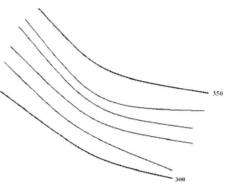

metre interval. These thicker lines are known as index contour lines and are also the one's that would have the height narrative alongside.

As above the height between contour lines is 10 (15) metres In areas with wide spaces between the lines this does not mean that the ground is flat. What it does mean is that the land in between has not reached the height level of the next contour. The land itself can be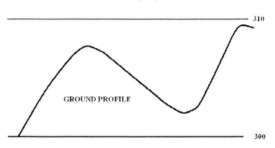

quite undulating in between the two lines.

In effect there may be a number of climbs of 9.99 metres without moving up to the next contour line. This can also mean that some features can get "lost" off the map because they fall below the 10 metres criteria. One example of this is small crags or earthworks.

This can also mean that you can put a substantial amount of climbing in without raising to the next contour line.

At times it can be difficult to tell whether the slope as shown by the contour lines is moving upwards or down. One helpful tip is that the top of the height narrative on the index contour is always on the up-slope of the ground.

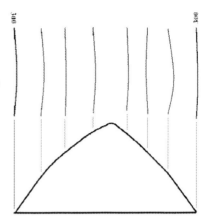

Being able to visualise and interpret contour lines and recognise the shape of the land is a vital skill in the art of navigation. It is important to be able to see the three dimensions of the landscape,
Specifically
1.    The height
2.    The steepness, and
3.    The profile.

The height is given by referring to the number of contour lines. The more lines, the greater the height, the more climbing there is. The index contour can be used to give a numerical value to the climb. If you are starting on the 300 metre line and going up to the 500 metre line, then you are obviously climbing 200 metres.

The steepness of the slope is given by how closely packed the contour lines are. As explained previously, the closer they are then the steeper the slope. It is extremely important to develop an awareness of the steepness of slopes by referring to the density of the contour lines. If necessary it is something that needs to be practised.

The profile of the ground, i.e. the different landforms that make up the hillsides, valleys, spurs, ridges and re-entrants, is made by the distinctive contour patterns. Recognising these patterns allows the navigator to imagine the shape of the land.

The diagrams below illustrate some of the more familiar contour patterns.

As an aid to reading contour lines try looking at other features. Streams run in the bottom of valleys while marshes and bogs are normally found in low-lying areas. On the other hand the summits of hills and ridges are usually absent of water features.

## Ridge

The contours rise closely-grouped together to meet on either side of a flatter area. This indicates a fairly level ridge. If the contours meet into a "V" shape then the 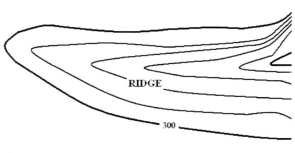 ridge is climbing. The sharper the point of the "V" then the narrower the ridge is.

## Valley

The contours form a vague "V" or "U" shape heading uphill. The valley floor, itself, is the opposite to a level ridge with the closely-grouped contours going up from either side of a flatter area. A valley may often contain a stream. Broad valleys and other flat areas make prime water catchment points. They collect the rainwater that flows off the surrounding hills.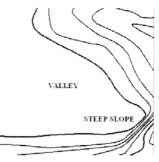

Easy to identify because of their lack of contours and the fact that there are often streams located close by.

## Summit

Most summits have some form of "furniture" possibly a trig point, cairn, stone shelter or a memorial. In some cases it may even be a form of construction such as an aerial or radar station. However, sometimes the summit of a hill may not so easy to identify. On a map, its shown as the highest point within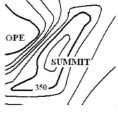

43

the topmost contour ring. If there is no trig point shown then there is usually a spot height within the ring. This is normally the summit but not always.

If the summit is not marked then it can be up to nine metres above the height of the last contour line.

## Cliff

Normally shown on maps as a well-defined line of tight, square-shaped outcrops. The contours will be very closely grouped. They may be that tightly grouped that due to lack of space, some lines may be omitted.

Note that not all cliffs may be shown on the map - always watch your contours.

## Col or saddle

A col, saddle or hause, as it is known in the Lakes, is the lowest point between two joined hills. In silhouette it would look as follows.

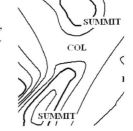

## Re-entrant

A re-entrant is a small shallow valley. Quite often it will only be one contour line high. The re-entrant is a course setter's favourite and is often the site for controls.

## Spur

A spur is simply a small ridge perhaps only one or two contour levels high.

## Platform

A shelf-like feature, a small flat area normally part way up a slope.

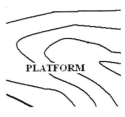

44

Now lets see how this would all look on the one diagram.

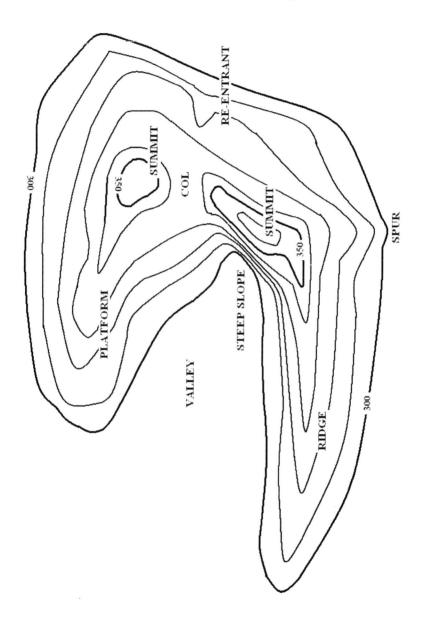

# Concave and convex slopes

As you would expect the majority of slopes do not have a uniform angle, the gradient alters as you move up or down the slope. However the shape of the slope can affect the gradient which in turn can affect route choice decisions.

Generally speaking a concave slope steepens as it rises. The gradient starts off shallow and then gradually steepens as you move up the hill. This is shown by the volume of the contour lines which are more closely packed nearer to the top of the slope.

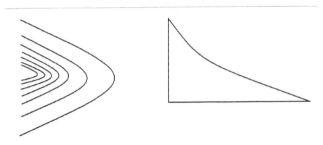

In contrast a convex slope is the reverse, the slope steepens as it falls. The gradient starts off shallow at the top of the hill and then increases as you move downwards. Again, the volume of the contour lines will be more closely packed nearer to the bottom of the slope.

Where this becomes relevant is in anticipating what is coming next particularly with convex slopes. Be wary when descending off-path routes down convex slopes unless you are sure of the ground. From the top you will probably not be able to see dangerously steep ground and, once there, there is always the temptation to try and find a way down, putting yourself in more trouble, rather than climb back up to find a safer route. This can be particularly dangerous in times of bad weather such as heavy rain, snow and ice when the danger of slipping is particularly high.

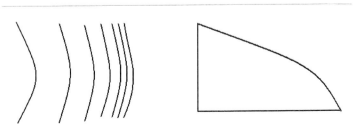

# Line features

Line features are, as the name suggests, features that run in a line across the face of the map. Examples are roads, tracks, paths, walls, fences, rivers, streams and ditches. These features are easy to identify on the map and, even more importantly, easy to identify and follow on the ground. They can lead you from one point to another with very little risk of getting lost.

The use of line features is a fundamental part of navigation and is used in a number of techniques such as rough navigation, handrail and aiming-off and also as catching features.

Because line features are easy to identify on the map and easy to follow on the ground their use is very simple. However don't underestimate simple. Simple navigation is fast navigation and they should be used as much as possible. Get into the habit of trying to identify line features on the map and try to follow them to as close to the target/control as possible.

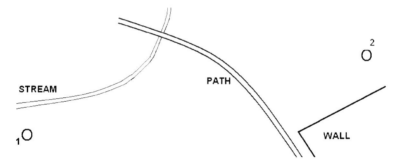

Often following line features can take you relatively close to your target without any complicated navigation, such as in the situation above when going from control 1 to control 2.

Quite often the following of line features to the destination will result in travelling a longer distance than the straight line route. However due to the ease with which they can be followed the running time may actually be faster despite the extra distance.

With some line features such as paths and tracks, it is possible to get congested areas where, for example, a number of paths run through a small area. In this case it becomes important to be able to distinguish the correct line feature both on the map and on the ground. If necessary use the

47

compass to establish that the feature is heading in the same direction as the one that you want.

It is possible to view a number of individual features as a line feature if they are set-out appropriately. For example, grouse butts are normally set out in a line which can be used as a handrail especially as there is normally a path in-between linking them together.

Line features should not be misinterpreted as contour lines or features. Contours are the only things shown on the map in brown.

# Contour features

As we said previously, contour lines are lines drawn across the map to show the height and shape of the land. As such most of the time these lines are shown as smooth sweeping lines. However, occasionally this smooth sweep of the landscape is interrupted by a feature that either jumbles the contour lines together or distorts the following line. These are readily identifiable and are known as contour features. They are features that are formed by the contour lines.

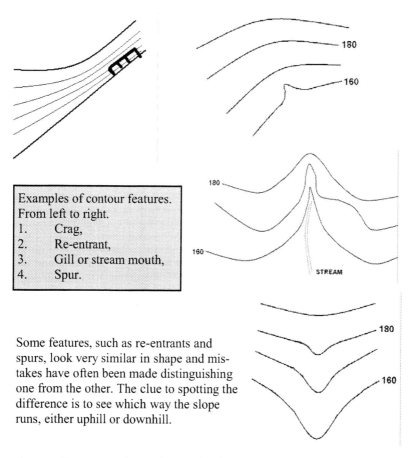

Examples of contour features.
From left to right.
1.      Crag,
2.      Re-entrant,
3.      Gill or stream mouth,
4.      Spur.

Some features, such as re-entrants and spurs, look very similar in shape and mistakes have often been made distinguishing one from the other. The clue to spotting the difference is to see which way the slope runs, either uphill or downhill.

Contour features can be used as navigational tools. The larger, more visible ones can be used as tick-off features (see Section 7 Fundamental Skills). The smaller ones such as re-entrants, spurs and platforms are often used as control sites. Because the skill is in recognising a landform as opposed to seeing a physical object such as a boulder, they can be quite difficult to locate.

Some of these contour features are not very large and may only be one or two contour lines high.

**Using contour features as handrails or line features.**
With some contour features it is possible to use them as if they were line features and as a result they can then become handrails or even catching features. This is obviously difficult if there is just the one feature in isolation but where there are a number in a rough line this then becomes possible.

**Examples of using contour features as handrails.**

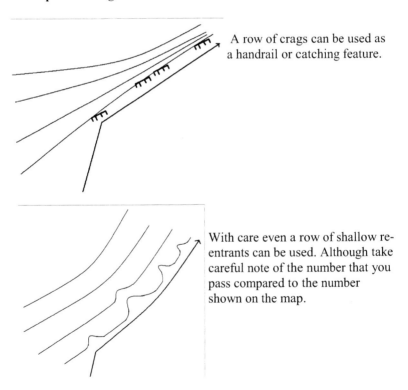

A row of crags can be used as a handrail or catching feature.

With care even a row of shallow re-entrants can be used. Although take careful note of the number that you pass compared to the number shown on the map.

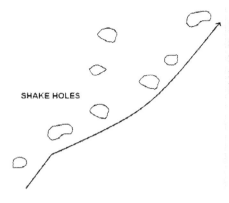

SHAKE HOLES

Even something as unlikely as shake holes can be used. All it needs is something that can be recognised on the map and can be recognised on the ground.

Land forms not sufficiently high enough to warrant a contour line can also be used as a line feature/handrail. In this case a line of spoil heaps helps maintain course while contouring across a slope. Note that if using such a feature it is normally best to check with a compass that it does run in the right direction and does not deviate away from the line of travel.

# Point features

Point features are features that are normally less than a few metres across. Examples of these are boulders, pits, depressions, platforms, knolls, crags, ruins and buildings.

Whether these are shown on the map will be dependant upon the amount of detail the map shows. The OS 1:50,000 will generally not show many of these items with the exception of buildings. The Harvey's map, being a specialist outdoor map, will tend to show them all. The OS 1:25,000 falls in-between.

Because of their small area, point features are normally more difficult to locate. For this reason they are always a favourite of the course planner for locating controls.

Small boulder. An example of a visible point feature, in this case a control on a permanent orienteering course.

Depression. With it being below ground level, a not so visible point feature. Normally depressions are not singular and you will find a number of them within a certain area which increases the difficulty of locating a specific one.

# Symbols on maps

Maps use a system of symbols to represent objects found on the ground. These can range from roads to lakes to marshes. Unfortunately all three major map types use different variations of symbol for the same object. This can lead to some confusion especially when one map type shows some objects that another does not. The table below gives an indicator of what is included on OS and Harvey's maps.

With regard to understanding symbols, the best advice is to identify which type of map is going to be used on the event or in training and

| Symbol | OS 1:25,000 | Harvey's 1:40,000 | OS 1:50,000 |
|--------|-------------|-------------------|-------------|
| Road | Yes | Yes | Yes |
| Track or forest road | Yes | Yes | Yes |
| Footpath | Yes | Yes | Yes |
| Intermittent footpath | No | Yes | No |
| Railway | Yes | Yes | Yes |
| Buildings | Yes | Yes | Yes |
| Ruin or sheepfold | Yes | Yes | No |
| Trig point | Yes | Yes | Yes |
| Maintained boundary wall or fence | Yes | Yes | No |
| Ruined boundary wall or fence | No | Yes | No |
| Scree | Yes | Yes | Yes |
| Loose rock/boulders | Yes | Yes | No |
| Large single boulder | No | Yes | No |
| Large cairn | No | Yes | No |
| Large crag | Yes | Yes | Yes |
| Outcrop of rock | Yes | Yes | Yes |
| Footbridge | Yes | Yes | Yes |
| Lake | Yes | Yes | Yes |

| Symbol | OS 1:25,000 | Harvey's 1:40,000 | OS 1:50,000 |
|---|---|---|---|
| River | Yes | Yes | Yes |
| Wide stream | Yes | Yes | Yes |
| Stream | Yes | Yes | Yes |
| Marsh | Yes | Yes | No |
| Peat hag | No | Yes | No |
| Coniferous forest | Yes | Yes | Yes |
| Deciduous forest | Yes | Yes | Yes |
| Dense forest | No | Yes | No |
| Firebreaks | Yes | Yes | No |
| Improved pasture | No | Yes | No |
| Rough pasture | Yes | Yes | No |
| Public footpath | Yes | Yes | Yes |
| Public bridleway | Yes | Yes | Yes |
| Public telephone | Yes | Yes | Yes |
| Mountain rescue kit | Yes | Yes | No |

memorise the relevant symbol table.

As can be seen there is a great deal more relevant information concerning point features and ground terrain on a Harvey's map than the corresponding OS one. In an event where navigation skills are tested such as a mountain marathon, then any map provided by the organisers will usually be a Harvey's.

Information on recognising ground types and using this information is included in the Section 10 Route Choice.

# Boundaries

There are two types of boundary shown on a map.

1. Field boundaries, and
2. Administrative boundaries.

## Field Boundaries

Field boundaries are one of the most useful features on a map, They are the lines that separate one field from another and are shown on the map by a thin solid black line. Unfortunately there is no differentiation as to whether the boundary is a fence, hedge or wall. In certain circumstances, such as on a moor, it can even be just an earth bank. However the fact that there is something there that is distinguishable on the map and on the ground is a great aid to navigation.

With regard to maps, be aware that both the OS 1:25,000 and Harvey's 1:40,000 maps show field boundaries but the OS 1:50,000 does not show sufficient detail and does not include them.

One problem with field boundaries is that they can always change. Hedges, fences and walls can all be removed and new ones planted and built. This means that it is always possible for part of a map to be out of date.

However, bearing this in mind, with practise it is very easy to recognise the shapes and lines of the boundaries on the map and on the ground.

Quite often, especially in lowland areas, field boundaries are bordered by drainage ditches. This means that there is a blue line next to the black boundary line. Be aware that at times one can conceal the other and lead to confusion.

## Administrative Boundaries

Because OS maps are meant to be general purpose they contain information that is of value to some user groups but not others. A prime example of this is administrative boundaries. These are the boundary lines between different administrative governing bodies such a county and parish councils.

For the outdoor person these boundaries are not of any special interest. However, because of their prominence on the map and the fact that they can be very easily confused with paths then they do become of concern in order to avoid any errors in navigation. More than one person has tried to follow the line of a parish boundary thinking that it was a path.

Don't ignore the boundary lines that are shown in the information box. Learn to differentiate between them and the other more useful information shown on the map.

# Other items shown on maps

As well as the symbols, maps show other information which is named on the map. Sometimes this name/description is not quite self-explanatory. Below is a list of terms commonly used and a description. Be aware that this list is not exhaustive and that there may be others out there that are not listed.

### Shake Hole
A depression in a limestone landscape caused by water eroding the limestone from underneath causing the ground surface to collapse downwards. Can vary a lot in terms of size and depth. These holes can sometimes be hidden by heather and other vegetation making them a potential hazard. In some cases they may also contain deep water. Not always identified individually on the map but if they are shown by a small circle with the narrative "Shake Hole" alongside , more often shown in a group as "Area of Shake Holes".

### Grouse Butt
A man-made hide for grouse shooters. Comes in a variety of sizes, shapes and constructions. Shown on the map as a dot but not normally found as a single feature, will tend to be laid out in a line, one after the other with the narrative "Grouse Butts". A useful feature to use for a handrail or a catching feature (see Section 9 Techniques ). However be aware that estate management is faster moving than Ordinance Survey and it is totally possible to have a new row of grouse butts that are not shown on the map and also butts that are shown on the map that will no longer exist on the ground.

### Tumulus
Written on the maps in an old-fashion style. They are an ancient burial mound normally pre-dating roman times. Although a mound, they can vary in height with some being barely noticeable at all. Usually found at locations that give a good viewpoint over the surrounding country. If prominent they can be a very useful navigation tool particularly as an attack point.

### Bell Pit  + Pits + Shafts
Holes and shafts in the ground left over from old mining activity. A bell pit is a bell-shaped hole, wider at the bottom than the top. Always be wary of these as not all are fenced or even covered. Shown on the map as a small circle with the appropriate narrative alongside i.e. "Shaft".

## Boundary Stones
Often shown as a dot with the narrative "BS" on the OS map. They are a line of stones erected to signify a boundary line. Normally erected a couple of hundred years ago the boundary line itself may have no particular relation to anything today. The stones themselves may be of any height although they are usually smaller than waist height. The distance between stones also varies although quite often one stone can be seen from another but this is not always the case. Can be used as a catching feature but be aware that if the stones are not particularly large then they can be difficult to see.

## Cairns
Normally a man-made pile of stones. They are made for a variety of purposes ranging from memorials to navigation aids in bad weather. Some are more substantial than others. They can range from something that is several metres thick at the base and are taller than a man to others which are just a couple of dozen stones high. Shown on the map as a dot with the narrative "Cairn" however not all cairns are shown on the map nor does the map give any indication of size. Because they are basically just a pile of stones, they are relatively easy to construct and also to take back down. Meaning that there is always a question mark about their permanency. They can be a very useful navigation tool.

## Curricks
Similar to cairns only larger. This makes them a lot more permanent. However bear in mind that over the years some of these curricks may have had some of their stones removed or been damaged and as a result may be smaller than what you are expecting. Like cairns shown on the map as a dot with the word "Currick" alongside.

## Sheepfolds
An enclosure for holding sheep. Normally built of stone. Can vary in size with some of them being quite substantial, very easy to see in normal visibility. Shown as a small circle with the narrative "Sheepfold" alongside however, physically they may be any shape and not necessarily the circle as shown on the map. A good navigation tool as either an attack point or as a tick-off feature along a route.

## Footbridge
Marked on maps as two small black lines crossing the water course with the letters "FB" alongside. As the name suggests a bridge over a stream or river that is only suitable for pedestrians.

## Shops

Strange to see shops marked on the map in the middle of no-where. A shop was the name of a lodging house for miners especially in the North Pennines. Nowadays they are mostly ruins but some have been restored and are used as shooting huts. As most of these shops have names they are identified on the map by their name, i.e. Yad Moss Shop.

Quite useful to use as attack points or as a shelter during rest stops. In a lot of cases there is usually a network of small paths around them either from the days when they were actually being used or created by sheep seeking shelter round the buildings/ruins. These are not normally shown on the map so take care if you use them and check to ensure that they are actually taking you in the right direction.

## Hush

A hush is another relic from the old mining days and is a reminder of the less environmentally-friendly methods used for ore extraction. The method was simply to build a dam at the head of a stream and when sufficient water pressure was built up, release it to wash the top soil away and expose the ore-bearing rock underneath. The normal result is a small steep-sided valley, very much like a gouge in the ground. Usually these are too small to be shown on the map by contour lines and they are indicated by shaded black lines with the narrative "Hush" alongside. Some hushes may be named.

Can be useful to use as a collecting feature or a line feature. However, be aware that if you are planning to cross them or travel down them, then they can be very steep sided and crossing or using them may not be as fast as you would wish. Because contour lines are not normally used to indicate them, then there is often no way to judge how deep they are and the exertion required to cross them.

## Waterfall

The name obviously describes what it is. Shown on the map as a single black line crossing the blue line of the water course. If it exists, the name of the waterfall will be alongside it as part of the narrative i.e. "White force Waterfall". When there is no name then the map will just say "Waterfall".

Often it is difficult to judge the size of the waterfall from the map and some of them may only be two or three metres high.

# Magnetic Variation

The earth is similar to a giant magnet and creates its own magnetic field. If a magnetised object, such as a compass needle, is suspended in the magnetic field then it will align itself with the magnetic north pole. This is the basic principle behind using a compass to give a constant reference point irrespective of where you are, i.e. magnetic north.

However as we have seen previously, the grid lines on a map are based on the national grid. North as shown on a map does not coincide with the magnetic north pole but rather with grid north. Grid north and magnetic north are not the same thing..

This issue is further complicated due to the fact magnetic north is not a fixed point. Over the course of a number of years it does change it's position. Fortunately this movement can be predicted which allows the difference between grid north and magnetic north to be tracked. Currently (2007) the difference between the two is around 3 degrees. By 2015 it has been calculated that this difference will be close to zero.

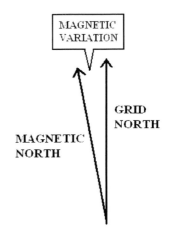

We, therefore, have a situation where the compass is pointing to a different north compared to the grid north as shown on a map, an allowance, known as magnetic variation, has to be made when using map and compass together.

When taking a bearing, we are establishing the direction of travel as an angle away from north. With having two north's, grid north and magnetic north, although the direction of travel

**Point to Note.**
Ordnance Survey and Harvey's maps both have their grid lines orientated to grid north. Therefore magnetic variation would apply when converting bearings from grid to magnetic and vice-versa.
If the event is using a specialist orienteering map then you will find that the grid lines are orientated to magnetic north. This saves the orienteer having to mess around with magnetic variation.

will be constant, the angle from north will differ, dependant upon which north you use. As magnetic north is to the west of grid north in the UK, the magnetic or compass bearing will always be the greater of the two. The difference between the two being the magnetic variation.

It is possible to convert bearings from a grid bearing to a magnetic bearing and vice-versa. To convert from grid to magnetic, add the variation. To convert from magnetic to grid, subtract the variation. Remember the phrase "grid to mag, add : mag to grid, get rid".

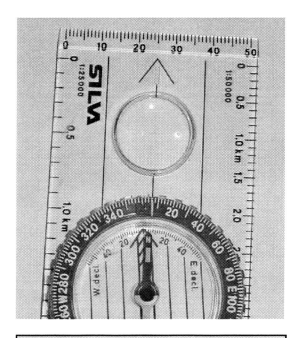

Adjusting the compass for magnetic variation - three degrees anti-clockwise.

Watch out in some volcanic areas such as the Scottish Islands as strange movements can be caused on the compass by the magnetic qualities of the local rock.

Both OS and Harvey's maps indicate magnetic variation and show the angle between grid north and magnetic north in the map margin.

# The Importance of Trig Points.

Originally erected in Great Britain by Ordnance Survey in 1935, Trig points assisted in the accurate re-mapping of the whole country by triangulation. When all the trig points were in place, it was possible, in clear weather, to see at least two other trig points from any one trig point. Careful measurements of the angles between the lines-of-sight of the other trig points then allowed the construction of a system of triangles which could then be referenced back to a single baseline to construct a highly accurate measurement system.

Trig points are truncated square concrete pyramids or obelisks tapering towards the top. On the top a brass plate with three arms and a central depression is fixed. A plaque on the side provides the reference number of the trig point and the letters OSBM (Ordnance Survey Bench Mark). The trig point has concealed mountings for a specialised theodolite, which was temporarily mounted on the trig point while measurements were taken.

As with everything nowadays, modern technology has taken over and the OS use satellite position fixing. For map makers trig points are now redundant.

Marked on the map by a blue triangle, the trig point is still very useful to the navigator in many ways but namely.
- Confidence booster when found especially in poor visibility.
- Opportunity to re-calibrate your altimeter accurately.
- Can be used during route choice as a way-marker.
- Used for taking a bearing to or from.

Trig points are a welcome part of being in the hills and often as they are the top of the hill present a great time to stop, take in the view, contemplate the rest of the route and take on some drink and food.

# The Problem with Maps.

Maps are great, they make navigating unknown areas easy. However, they are not infallible. There can be problems with maps which can result in confusion and its best that you are aware of them.

1.  Maps are printed and as part of the printing process some objects may be over printed on to other objects thus obscuring them. For example, below, the public right of way has been printed on top of the line of the wall. In this case it makes it confusing as to whether the right of way is on the left hand or right hand side of the wall.

2.  Maps, in particular OS maps, are general purpose. They contain lots of information that is not relevant to the navigator. Some of this can obscure or can be confused with other more important bits of information. It is beneficial to have an understanding of all the symbols used on a map.

3.  Maps don't contain all the information that would be beneficial to the navigator. Sometimes due to problems with scale some items are omitted. An obvious example of this are small crags. Smaller crags can fall just under the contour height interval. As such they are not large enough to warrant being included as a crag on the map even though they do exist on the ground.

4.  Land management can be a fast moving environment. Things can exist on the ground that do not exist on the map and vice-versa. Examples can be new tracks or roads built by estate management, new bridges over streams and even plantations removed by felling.

5.  The map may show a public right of way such as a footpath or bridleway. In reality this does not mean that there is actually a path on the ground. The path may be totally non-existent or overgrown with vegetation.

6.  Maps are one dimensional. It can be difficult trying to visualise the size and shape of the land through contour lines.

7.  There are very clear differences in style between the OS maps and Harvey's. If you are not familiar with the scale and symbols of the type that you are using in competition then that can cause prob-

lems.

On the more practical side there can also be physical problems with maps.

8. Maps are quite bulky and not easy to carry. It can be quite awkward folding them down so that you only see the area that is relevant to you. In windy weather it can be a major operation folding a large size map especially if it is double sided and needs turning over.

9. Maps are printed on paper which although hard wearing is subject to wear and tear and will eventually fall apart especially if exposed to wet weather. They need to be protected from the elements.

10. When marking up routes the map can be difficult to write on especially in the open. There is also a limit to the number of times that you can write over the same map area with some degree of legibility. This shortens the working life of the map.

Maps are essential to navigation but be aware of their limitations and the problems that may give.

# 7. Fundamental Skills

In this section we will look at those basic skills that are the cornerstone of all navigation. These are the skills that you need. As discussed previously there are two schools of navigation for the runner. The first, where navigation is a tool to get you round a set route and the second, where testing the navigational ability is the main aim itself. With both of these styles the basic fundamental skills covered here are required.

1.    Understanding grid numbers.
2.    Plotting a grid reference onto a map.
3.    Setting the map.
4.    Taking a bearing.
5.    Keeping on course.
6.    Taking a back-bearing.
7.    Re-orientating.
8.    Thumbing the map.
9.    Using features to monitor progress.
10.   Leapfrogging.
11.   Reading the map while running.
12.   Memorising the map.

# Understanding Grid Numbers

If you look at any OS or Harvey's map you will see that it has a network of lines ( OS = blue, Harvey's = black ) going both up and down and across the map. These are grid lines and form part of the national grid system that covers the whole of mainland Britain.

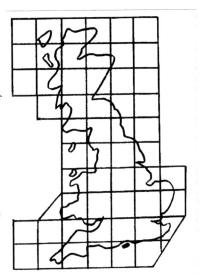

The grid is an index system that breaks the country down into a series of large squares 100 km x 100 km. Each of these 100 km squares has a two letter identification, for example NZ or NJ. These letters are normally found in the map margins.

Each of these large squares is then broken-down even further into smaller squares of 1 km x 1 km.

The grid lines shown on the map form the 1 km x 1 km squares. These grid lines are all numbered with the numbers being between 00 and 99 so that it is possible to refer to an individual square by using the numbers of the two lines which bound it on the west and the south.

It is important to understand that any four figure grid reference obtained from these numbered lines is duplicated in each of the 100 km squares. In order to make each individual grid reference unique, the two grid letters that identify the 100 km square need to be added, i.e. NZ 89 03.

The vertical grid lines are known as Eastings because they are numbered

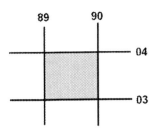

eastwards. When giving or reading a grid reference they are always given first. The horizontal lines are known as Northings because they are numbered northwards. The numbers of these lines are always given second in a grid reference. This would give you a four figure number that would identify an individual 1 km x 1 km square, for example 89 03.

Obviously a 1 km x 1 km square does not give a great deal of accuracy in locating a precise spot for navigation. In order to give this precision, a third figure can be added to each of the two digit grid references. The 1 km x 1 km squares are subdivided down into 100 metre squares by dividing the 1 km square side by 10. It is important to note that there are no grid lines printed on the map to represent this subdivision. However on the borders of the map, both the easting and the northing have the 1 km broken down in to ten as an aid to plotting the grid reference. In practical terms this may not be much use as to use them may involve folding and re-folding the map. This is where the use of a roamer comes in, see Section 4 Tools.

This subdivision now allows a six figure grid reference to be used. In the example 893 034.

It is worth noting that even when broken down to six figures, the grid reference only applies to a 100 metre x 100 metre grid square so you will still need to look for the feature described on the checkpoint sheet.

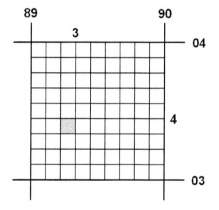

67

# Plotting a Grid Reference onto a Map

### Plotting the grid reference

To plot a 6-figure grid reference onto a map is another fundamental skill. Practice at home, you may be transferring a list of grid references onto a map in the wet with cold hands and mistakes cost time.

As an example, in the case below the grid reference 345 128 would look as follows. 345 is on the east/west axis while 128 is on the north/south axis.

When copying down checkpoints from a list or a master map always double check – we all have made mistakes. Even better get your partner to check.

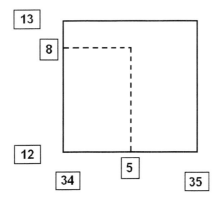

### Marking up the map.

The starting point for all navigation is knowing where you are and where you are going to. On all events whether it is a race or a mountain marathon style event you will be given a list of grid references which will be the locations of the checkpoints or controls. This makes navigation faster and easier.

The most common style of marking is the same one as used in orienteering and involves using circles.

The starting point is denoted by a pyramid

Checkpoints and/or controls by a circle

A partial circle may be used so as not to cover up the detail of a feature

The finish is denoted by a double circle or donut

In addition to this there may be areas of land that for one reason or another the organisers don't want you to cross. These are known as out-of-bounds areas. It is always best to mark these on the map to avoid inadvertently straying into them. This is normally done by hatching the area.

## Master maps.

Some events will use a "master map" system. This involves the use of a map known as the master map with all the controls and other relevant information such as out-of-bounds areas marked up on it. This is available for you to copy the location of the controls and other information from, on to either the map that has been provided or your own map. When copying down locations always take your time and be careful. And don't forget to double check. It can provide hours of endless fun trying to follow an incorrectly marked-up map.

On events where a map is provided, the location of the controls and other information may already be pre-printed on the map. However always check in case there is a master map with any last-minute alterations.

# Setting the Map

One of the first and most important techniques in navigation is setting or orienting the map. This is quite simply placing the map so that with your own position as the central point., all the features shown on the map are in their correct relative positions and aligned to the features actual positions in the landscape around you. Effectively laying it out in front of you in such a way that it resembles the ground in front..

This is done so that the terrain around you matches the map you are studying. This makes it easier to start identifying landmarks. You can then identify changes in direction, junctions and features that you will pass along your route. This will help confirm that you are on the correct route and also your position along the route.

When navigating the map should always be kept set. It makes life so much easier and it should become instinctive as soon as you pick up a map.

There will be times when you will find yourself reading an upside-down map, don't be put off by this. The map is supposed to reflect your physical surroundings. It doesn't matter about the words on the map. Most of them wouldn't be relevant to what you are doing anyway.

There are two methods of setting the map depending upon the level of visibility.

1. Setting the map by visual reference.
2. Setting the map by compass.


## 1.    Setting the map by visual reference.

Obviously the easiest and quickest method and the one that is used in most circumstances. Quite simply the map is aligned against a number of physical features that can be seen in the landscape.

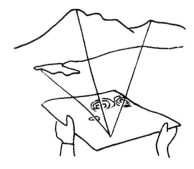

When following a linear feature such as a
path or a track, it is normally only necessary
to identify that one feature. Turn the map
until the path on the map lines up with the
real path that you are following.

## 2. Setting the map by compass.

This method is used to set the map
when there are no readily identifiable features visible. This may be
down to poor visibility such as low
cloud, mist etc, or just quite simply no visible features in the landscape.

The easiest way to do this is to
quite simply match the edge of the
compass with the north-south grid
line and turn both the map and the
compass until the red end of the
needle falls inside the housing arrow.

To get an exact setting of the map
it is possible to allow for magnetic
variation by either just turning the
map and compass that little bit
more or by setting the actual variation on the compass dial however,
in most circumstances a rough setting without the magnetic compen-
sation would be sufficiently accurate.

Setting the map should be done
often and become instinctive.

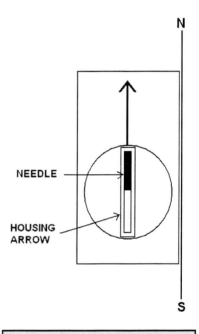

Setting the map by compass. Align
the north-south grid line along the
edge of the compass and turn map
and compass until the needle falls
within the housing arrow.

# Taking a Bearing

Other than setting the map, the compass can be an invaluable tool for telling you the direction to travel in. This is known as taking a bearing and is essentially using the angle between magnetic north and the desired direction of travel to guide you.

This technique comes into its own when
1. visibility is poor such as in thick mist,
2. when the landscape is featureless so that there is no defined visible features to guide you, and
3. when trying to locate a small feature.

With practise a very high level of accuracy can be obtained. The ability of taking a bearing should become an automatic action so that it isn't necessary to think how to do it.

There are four simple steps to taking and following a bearing.

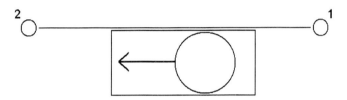

1. Place the compass on the map with the base plate edge running along a line from your starting point to your destination point.

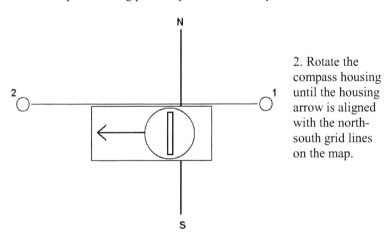

2. Rotate the compass housing until the housing arrow is aligned with the north-south grid lines on the map.

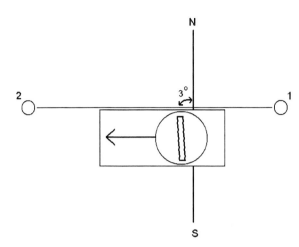

3. To allow for magnetic variation between grid north and magnetic north, turn the compass housing anti-clockwise by 3 degrees (in 2007, this figure will differ over time).

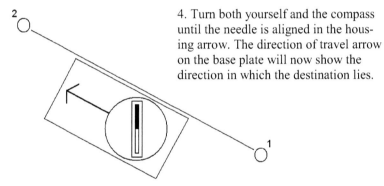

4. Turn both yourself and the compass until the needle is aligned in the housing arrow. The direction of travel arrow on the base plate will now show the direction in which the destination lies.

In certain circumstances travelling in a straight line between starting point and destination point may not be practical. This is normally due to obstacles such as lakes or cliffs in between. These can be avoided by using intermediate targets to "box" the obstacle. This is part of breaking a leg down into sections which is in Section 10 Route Choice.

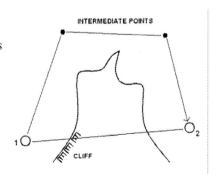

73

Care needs to be taken when sighting a bearing especially when you have to take multiple bearings on a long leg. Slight inaccuracies each time that you take the bearing can result in missing the target by several hundred metres.

## Following a rough bearing

The description above describes how to follow an accurate bearing. Sometimes there is no need to follow a bearing that accurately. There are times when crossing terrain when it does not matter whether you know exactly where you are. Use the bearing to point yourself roughly in the right direction and then run just checking every now and then that you are going roughly the right way. Further details on this technique are included in Section 8. Advanced Skills.

## Checking the direction of line features.

This can help in selecting the correct line feature and/or ensuring that a feature that you are following is heading in the right direction. This is done in four easy stages.

1.  Place the edge of the compass along the line feature on the map, with the direction of travel arrow pointing in the direction that you want to travel.
2.  Hold the map in front of you so that the direction of travel arrow points away and directly in front of you.
3.  Turn the housing so that the housing arrow aligns along the north/ south grid line.
4.  Turn so that the north end of the compass needle rests within the housing arrow. The direction of travel arrow will now be indicating the direction in which the line feature should be heading. If the line feature is not heading in that direction then it is the wrong feature.

## Problems with taking a bearing.

Maintaining a compass bearing, especially when running, is not an easy matter. Competitors often over-estimate their ability with a compass, it takes a good navigator to travel the relatively short distance of 400 metres on a compass bearing and still expect to come out exactly on target. The majority of navigators will be out by some degree.

# Keeping on Course

Once you have a bearing how do you ensure that you keep on course.

With reasonable visibility the easiest way is to just pick features that you can see lying along your direction of travel and just simply run towards them. Ideally the line of travel will have two or more features along it. Keeping these aligned will help avoid any drifting to one side of the line of travel.

With good visibility there should be little need to keep referring to the compass as you have a visible target that you are aiming for. This gives the advantage of being able to make adjustments for difficult terrain by running round it while still being able to keep your direction of travel.

In poor visibility this becomes more difficult as features become more difficult to see and line up. Teamwork then comes into play as two navigators can be better than one. With one partner checking the navigation of the other. In extremely poor visibility it may be necessary to use the leapfrogging technique (see later in this section).

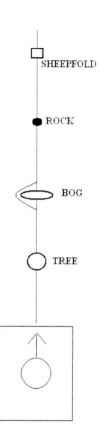

Running on a bearing across the line of slope is notoriously difficult as there is a natural tendency to drift down the slope. If you can focus on an object that is on your line of travel and head towards that, it will help prevent the drifting.

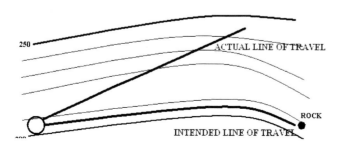

# Taking a Back-bearing.

This is a technique that can be used to locate your position on the map. To provide greater accuracy it is best used when you are on a line feature such as a stream or fence.

1.      Choose a feature from the landscape around you that you can easily identify on the map such as hill summit, forest edge or building.
2.      Point the direction of travel arrow at the feature. Holding the compass in this position, turn the housing until the housing arrow lies directly beneath the north end of the compass needle. The reading that is shown on the housing is your bearing.
3.      Subtract the magnetic variation from the bearing, i.e. 270 - 3 = 267, set this on the compass.
4.      Place the compass on the map so that the housing arrow aligns with the north-south grid lines.
5.      Move the compass on the map so that the edge intersects with the chosen feature.
6.      Draw a line along the edge and if necessary extend the line until it crosses the line feature that you are on.
7.      Your position is where the line crosses the line feature.

A more advanced form of using this technique can be used to locate your position in pathless terrain. This is known as Resection. See Section 8 Advanced Skills for more details.

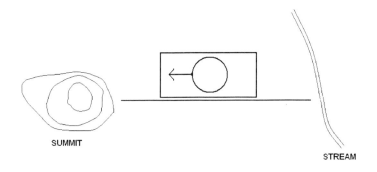

SUMMIT

STREAM

# Re-orienting.

At some time every navigator becomes lost or misplaced. How well you cope with this is the mark of a good navigator.

One of the main problems with getting lost is the fact that most people have a tendency to refuse to recognise when this has happened and will just continue in the hope that things will come right. Unfortunately this is not normally the case and the sooner that you recognise and accept the fact that you are misplaced then the easier it is to correct.

The first step when lost is to stop. Taking a straight forward and sensible approach will normally correct most mistakes. So orientate the map and try to relate the features on the ground in front of you to those shown on the map. Try to work out the route you might have taken from your last known position. This may enable you to make a slight adjustment to the route that you are following in order to bring you back on course.

If you are unable to figure out your position then try and head for a nearby prominent line feature. From there take a back-bearing on a visible feature and locate your position along the line feature. Once your position is known you should then be able to make a course correction to bring you back on route.

In the circumstances that you are still unable to locate your position then there is no other course of action other than trying to retrace your steps back to the point where you were last sure of your position. From there try again.

**So what are the clues to recognise when you are lost/misplaced.**
1.  The ground in front of you does not agree to the map.
2.  The handrail that you are following suddenly changes direction to that which you were expecting.
3.  It has been a period of time since you last passed a recognisable feature, or features that you expect to pass don't appear.

If any of these occur then the probability is that you have gone astray.

# Thumbing the Map

One of the key fundamental skills of navigation is to always know where you are. As such the good navigator will always have their map and compass to hand and not in the rucksack or bumbag.

However, even with having the map out and in front of you, it can be very difficult to keep a track of your position on the map as you travel along your route. As you run along your eyes will, quite naturally, move away from the map to focus on where you are running. This will mean that every time that you wish to look at the map, you will have to re-find your position on it.

One way round this is to use a technique known as thumbing the map. Quite simply this is keeping your thumb next to where you are on the map. By pace counting and observing the terrain and lie of the land it is possible to keep moving the thumb to give a constant reference of your position. This technique is used in conjunction with using map features to monitor your progress.

By having your thumb constantly on your current location this means that you don't have to waste valuable time having to re-locate yourself every time that you need to look at the map. This also reduces the risk of errors and subsequent "misplacement".

Using the thumb to keep a track of your position on the map as you progress along the route.

# Using Features to Monitor Progress.

As you navigate along your route you will pass a number of features. These features can be used to monitor your progress and tell you your position along the route.

Prior to starting your leg you can identify these features on the map and then as you pass them note your progress. These features are sometimes called "tick-off" features because you tick them off as you pass. Knowing where these features are and being able to confirm their position as you run reduces the risk of getting lost or straying off-course.

The features used can be :
1.      A crossed-over line feature such as a stream or a wall,
2.      A feature passed close-by such as a boulder, forest edge or crag,
3.      A feature passed at a distance such as a hill or a valley.

This technique is usually used in conjunction with thumbing the map with the position of the thumb being updated as you pass the relevant features.

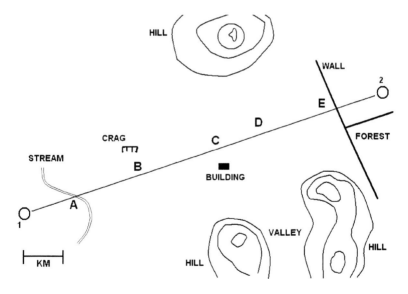

## Example of using features to monitor progress.
The distance from 1 to 2 is approx. 7 kms. As you run you can use the features passed to monitor your progress along the route and ensure that

you are still on track. By estimating distance and running speed you would have a good indication of when you would expect certain features to become visible. Assume 1 km equals six minutes running time.

After 1 km or six minutes you should be crossing a stream at point A.

After a further 1.25 km which would give you 2.25 kms or 13.5 minutes there should be a visible crag on the left point B.

Point C is a further 1.5 km giving a total running distance of 3.75 kms or 22.5 minutes and at this point there is a building visible on the right with a hill behind it.

Point D has a hill on the left side with a valley immediately opposite on the right. This is a total running distance of 4.75 kms from 1 or 28.5 minutes.

Point E is where the route crosses the wall at 6.25 kms from 1 or 37.5 minutes.

# Leapfrogging

Used when you need to follow a bearing in poor visibility when obvious marker points can't be identified. To put it quite simply, it's using your partner as a marker pole to aid your navigation.

1.  Take a bearing along your desired route.
2.  Send your partner off along this bearing until they are a reasonable distance away. This will depend upon visibility as they need to stay visible to you.
3.  Instruct your partner to move left or right in order to align themselves with the bearing.
4.  When satisfied that your partner is on the line of bearing, then join them.
5.  Repeat process until target is reached.

This technique takes time and will slow you down. However it is highly effective in poor visibility despite being slow and may save time rather than blundering about in the mist.

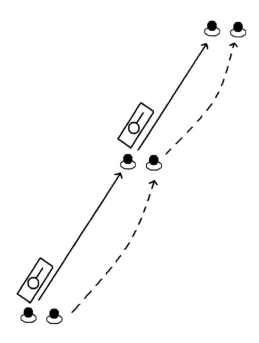

# Reading the Map While Running.

Being able to read the map while running is most definitely a natural skill. Can you do it, have you tried to do it ?

Most readings of the map are to check the runner's position and to do that most runners stop in order to take stock of their surroundings and then refer to the map. However if you can develop the skill of being aware of your surroundings at all times, then just a cursory glance at the map, especially if your thumb is marking your position, will confirm your location while still moving.

This is a skill that can be developed but it does need practice. However it will save time on all aspects of your navigation.

As you will note reading the map while running has a very close correlation with thumbing the map. Life becomes a whole lot easier when you use these skills together.

Being able to thumb the map and glance around you as you run will help keep a track of your position. Constant practice makes this task easier and eventually it will become second nature.

# Memorising the Map.

Obviously the less time you spend looking at the map then the faster you can run. If you can confidently and reliably remember sections of the route such as the features that you pass, the attack point description and also what the control is, then it can speed up your running time considerably.

However, this is not a case of remembering the whole map but rather just relevant pieces of it that relate to the leg that you are crossing.

Unfortunately memory retention is unique to the individual. However, with practise it can be developed. Try the memory exercises in Section 14 Training and Exercises.

**Notes**
If you do have problems with the memory there is nothing wrong with writing notes on the map or even separate route notes, as long as you don't write them in a place where they will interfere with your map reading. In fact it can be quite useful to write the letters of the control kite next to the control site that you have marked on the map. Saves double-checking with the control list as you approach it.
This may also prove helpful as with the control list being on a separate piece of paper it is possible to lose it.

# 8. Advanced Skills.

We've looked at the fundamental skills which any competent navigator should be familiar with and capable of performing. In this section we'll look at a few more advanced skills which, although aren't strictly necessary, will take your navigation to a higher level of competency. For those runners who only use their navigation for making their way round routes and courses knowledge of these skills will make them safer in the wilder places. With those runners where competitive navigation is the thing then these skills can become essential and can provide the difference between you and the competition.

1.  Rough and fine navigation.
2.  Attack points.
3.  Estimating slope angle.
4.  Resection.
5.  Estimating distance using pacing.
6.  Estimating distance using time.
7.  Estimating distance by eye.
8.  Which technique to use for estimating distance.

# Rough and Fine Navigation

## Rough navigation

Rough navigation is a technique used when it is not vital to know your exact position. Normally this is used during the first part of a leg when you are moving from one control to the attack point for the next.

When following a bearing you will find that it will be necessary to make frequent stops to check your position and the bearing. Even when you are moving, progress will be slow as you will not want to jolt the compass about. This all takes time and increases the time spent on any particular leg. If you can reduce the amount of stopping and checking and speed up your progress then your leg time will be reduced.

Rough navigation does this because there is no requirement to know exactly where you are. If you aim your course towards a feature that you are unlikely to miss then all the stopping and checking becomes unnecessary and the time taken to complete the leg will be reduced. The aim of rough navigation is to cover the ground as quickly as possible.

With this technique you use large and easily recognisable features especially line and catching features. This will involve using rough compass work and running on the needle and occasionally pace counting.

Rough navigation will include.

### Rough map reading
This is keeping map reading at the basics and using the largest, most easily recognised features available. If it is large it is visible, you don't have to waste time looking for it.
At the start of the leg identify any major features that you will follow or cross. Tick these off as you cross or pass them. It will help maintain your rough position.

### Rough compass work
Because you don't need to be heading on a precise bearing you can use a compass to just ensure that you are heading in the correct general direction.

## Example 1

Heading towards a stream.
Is it vital to know whether you are at point A or point B ?
As long as you are heading in the correct direction you will pick up the stream. It therefore becomes unnecessary to constantly stop and check and re-check your position. This will make the travelling time much faster.

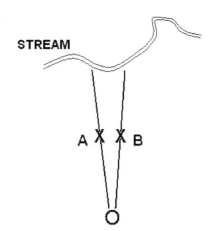

## Example 2

From checkpoint 1 take a rough compass bearing to point you in the right direction. It doesn't matter if you are at point A or point B. The large crag will be visible for most of the leg and if you ensure that you don't cross the stream then you know that you are going in the right direction.

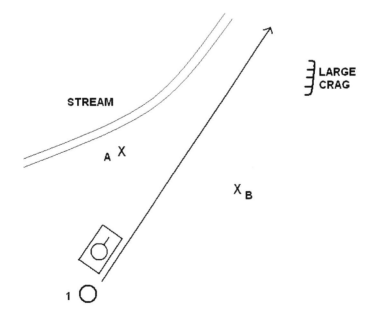

# Fine navigation

In contrast to rough navigation, fine navigation is the technique that you use when you need to know precisely where you are. This is the technique that is normally used in navigating from the attack point to the control.

Fine navigation involves accurate compass work following a bearing with the possible use of pacing out a number of steps to get the distance correct and get to the checkpoint precisely. It will also involve detailed map reading and/or a combination of both.

Because of the precise nature of fine navigation there are the following downsides.
1.      It is slower and takes more time than rough navigation, and
2.      There is a greater margin of error because you are aiming for an exact spot rather than a general area.

Therefore the more that you can reduce the need for fine navigation by using line features, catching features and rough navigation then the faster you will be able to run a leg. However there is a balance to be had. Failure to slow down and use the fine techniques as you approach a control can make you miss it and lose a lot of time. Gaining this balance is a result of experience and training.

The aim of fine navigation is to find the control. Unlike rough navigation it does not matter about the speed, or lack of it, at which you travel. Missing the control will normally cost more time than that spent while being slow and careful.

Fine navigation will involve.

## Slowing down
As was said above, the crucial element in fine navigation is being prepared to slow down and be careful and meticulous about what you are doing.

## Fine map reading
With fine navigation it is important to know where you are and what is around you at all times. This requires continuous contact with the map and the landscape and the use of every feature, large and small, to monitor progress and ensure that you are on course.

## Fine compass work
Unlike rough navigation, this involves taking an accurate bearing. To do

this will involve standing still and taking a great deal of care when sighting.

Even when fine map reading the compass should be used to check your heading.

## Pace counting

With fine navigation accuracy is crucial and guesses about distance estimation wouldn't work. Use pace counting to judge how far you need to go and how far you have gone.

So far we have said that there is rough navigation and fine navigation. The aim of rough navigation is to travel as fast as possible and the aim of fine navigation is to travel as accurately as possible. Unfortunately the two are mutually exclusive, you can do one or the other, you can't do both.

This means that at some point there is a switch-over from rough navigation to fine navigation. This normally happens around the attack point. However, in reality what does happen is that you have a "grey area" between the two when you begin to anticipate reaching the attack point. Although you are still following rough navigation principles, you begin to slow down and become more aware of surrounding features and their relationship with the map. In effect you are becoming more careful so that you don't miss the attack point.

## Combining rough and fine navigation.

Use rough navigation to get from checkpoint 1 to the wall. This may be done by taking a rough bearing and heading towards the stream. The stream is one km from the starting point so after approximately six minutes you should arrive at it.

Continue on the same rough bearing. By now the crag should be visible on the left. Pass the crag as close as possible but maintaining it's position on the left. The wall will soon come into view.

When you arrive at the wall you wouldn't know your exact position along it but does that matter. You will know that when you reach the wall you turn right and follow it to the attack point at the wall corner.

As you follow the wall you will be making the transaction from rough nav to fine nav. You will be slowing down and trying to anticipate what is coming ahead. Pay close attention to the wall just in case the corner is not as prominent as you would expect. What the map shows may not necessarily be what exists on the ground.

From the wall corner you will be using fine navigation techniques. At the corner stand still and take a bearing to the cairn. Measure the distance to the cairn with your pacing scale and then slowly set-off towards the cairn. As you progress compare the small features that you pass with those shown on the map, at the same time count your paces. When you reach the appropriate number you should be at the cairn.

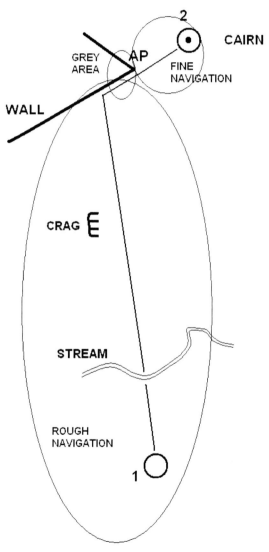

# Attack Points.

In events that test your navigation abilities, you'll find that most controls will not necessarily be on line features. That would be too easy. Instead they tend to be more isolated, standing on their own away from any easily recognised feature.

This means that to hit the control, precise navigation is needed. As we have now know precise navigation is slow and takes time. The longer the distance that you have to use precise (fine) navigation, then the longer the time taken to complete that particular leg.

So how can this time be reduced. The most effective way is by using what is known as an attack point. An attack point is an easily recognised point that is close to the control and can be used as the launch platform for the fine navigation that is then used to precisely locate the control. The attack point will then give either :

1. A short distance that you can measure and take a bearing.
2. You can then transfer to a technique such as handrail for the final short distance.

Because they are easily recognised, they are easier to find, meaning that rough navigation can be used to locate them and as we know, rough navigation is faster.

They are normally on a line feature such as a path junction, a stream bend, a wall corner etc. It is something that is easily and accurately found. If the control is more than 30 metres away from the attack point then it will normally be necessary to use the compass and possibly intermediate features to avoid missing the control.

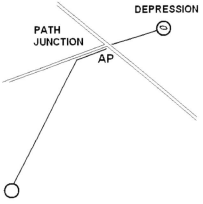

## Examples of attack points.

### Example 1.
Use rough navigation and the aiming-off technique (see Section 9 Techniques) to find the path junction. This then becomes the attack point for the final stretch to the control.

90

Take a bearing from the junction and if necessary, pace count to locate the depression.

### Example 2.
Taking a bearing directly from 1 to 2 gives the opportunity to miss the cairn at 2 or it will use a lot of time using fine navigation over a long distance.
Instead use rough navigation and the aiming-off technique to arrive at the wall corner. This can then be used as the attack point to take a bearing and precisely navigate the shorter distance from the corner to the cairn.
This will be a lot faster than navigating directly from 1 to 2 and with less chance of error.

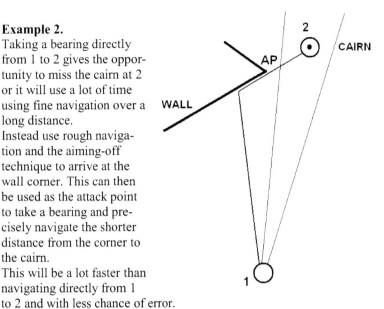

### Example 3.
Again using fine navigation to travel all the way from 1 to 2 would mean the leg taking a long time. Plus any error in taking a bearing could lead you to the wrong depression.
Instead use rough navigation and aiming-off to arrive at the stream junction.

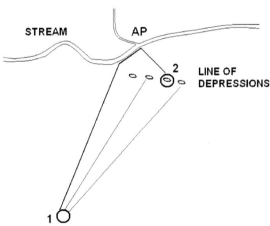

The junction can then be used as the attack point for approaching the correct depression.

## Example 4.

The small boulder at 2 would be difficult to see and travelling on a bearing directly from 1 carries a severe risk of missing the control altogether. On the other hand the crag will be much more prominent and will be quite likely visible from a distance. Use rough navigation and running on the needle to locate the crag and then use this as your attack point and from there take a bearing to the small boulder.

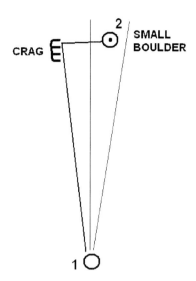

# Estimating Slope angle.

Knowing the angle of the slope that you are on is a rarely used but useful tool for locating your position.

Sometimes known as "aspect of slope" this technique uses the angle or slope of the hillside to locate your position. Not often used but a very useful tool, in featureless terrain this sometimes can be the only practical method of establishing your position.

The basic technique is to recognise the steepness and position of the slope and to then identify it on the map.

First it is useful to understand the steepness of the slope, the more contour lines per centimetre on the map then the steeper the slope.

| 1:25000 Contours per cm | Slope Angle in degrees |
|:---:|:---:|
| 5 | 50 |
| 4 | 40 |
| 3 | 30 |
| 2 | 20 |
| 1 | 10 |

Estimating slope angle is more accurate on a curved slope with good visibility. Although in misty conditions, if you can see enough to tell that the slope falls in a consistent direction then it should still work.

1.  The first step is to establish the "fall line" of the slope. This is the line that you or a ball would follow if rolled downhill. In theory this should be at

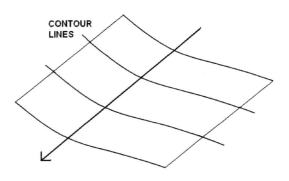

CONTOUR LINES

right angles to the contour lines.

2.  Take a compass bearing of this fall line.

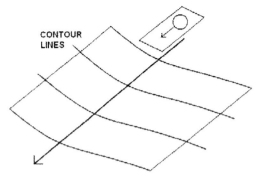

3.  Place the compass on the map and rotate the whole compass until the north lines are aligned with the north-south grid lines on the map.

4.  Hold the compass in this orientation and slowly move it across the map until you find either a point or points where the contour lines cross the edge of the compass at right angles.

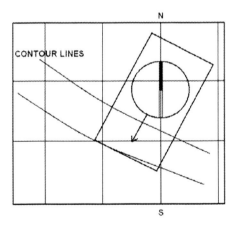

5.  Your position should be on one of these points.

# Resection .

In open, featureless country it can sometimes be difficult to judge your position. Resection is a method of locating your position and, if repeated, of keeping track of your movements, as you progress along the route.

To perform a resection you need at least two but preferably three identifiable features, that are not exactly opposite each other. In the example below a tarn, a hill top and a wood are used.

1.  Choose the three features from the landscape around you that you can identify on the map. Make sure that none of these features are directly opposite each other and that you are slightly off-set and not directly between two of the features (see diagram below).
2.  Point the direction of travel arrow at one of the features. Holding the compass in this position, turn the housing until the housing arrow lies directly underneath the north end of the compass needle. The reading that is shown on the housing is your bearing.
3.  Subtract the magnetic variation from the bearing obtained i.e. 280-3 = 277. And set this on the compass.
4.  Place the compass on the map so that the housing arrow aligns with the north-south grid lines.
5.  Move the compass on the map so that the edge intersects with the features. Draw a line along the path of this edge. Your position is along this line.
6.  Repeat this progress with the other two features, drawing a line from each of them.

In all probability the three lines will not meet at a point. However they will form a small triangle and your position will be in this triangle.

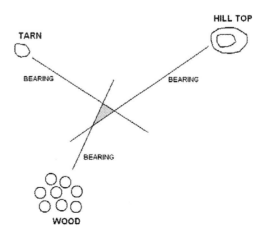

Resection can be a time-consuming procedure. While in poor visibility it is unlikely that you will even manage to see three features. In which case the chances of producing an accurate location is fairly slim.

## Locating your position when on a line feature .

If you are on a line feature this can make the task of performing a resection a whole lot easier. In this case all that you need is the one visible feature that you can identify on the map on which to take a bearing. You will know that you are somewhere along the line feature. Take a bearing from the visible feature in the same way as previously described, extend the line drawn from this bearing until it crosses the line feature. Where the two meet is your position.

This method is often known as taking a back-bearing.

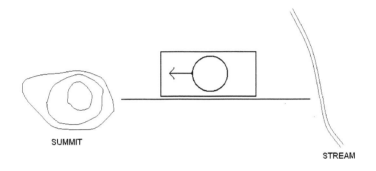

SUMMIT

STREAM

# Estimating Distance Using Pacing.

To put it simply, pace counting is counting the number of paces or steps used and then using that number to estimate the distance that you have travelled.

The first step to do this is to calculate how many paces it takes to cover a set of distance, i.e. 100 metres. To do this requires a tape measure or an accurate map. Measure out a hundred metres and then count the number of steps that it takes you to run this distance. Perform this exercise six times and work out the average number of steps to use as your pace count.

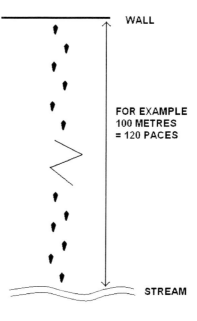

As an example, if we assume that it takes 120 steps to cover 100 metres then if you run for 60 steps then you have covered 50 metres and if you have run for 180 steps then you have covered 150 metres.

To use this in practice requires you to measure the distance from A to B from the map. That distance would then equate to a number of steps. Run from point A for the relevant number of steps and you should then be at point B.

To make the maths simpler some people use a pre-prepared pacing scale with the distance already measured-out in terms of numbers of paces. See below.

Pace counting is a simple and reliable method of judging distances. However it does have limitations. Pace counting is at it's most accurate on flat easy terrain at comfortable walking pace. You cannot pace count for 200 metres in poor visibility on rough terrain and expect to be within 30 metres of the correct distance.

1.    Pace counting is only accurate for short distances up to a couple of hundred metres.

2.  The faster you move the less accurate it is due to the varying stride length.
3.  The rougher or hillier the ground the less accurate it is.
4.  Your stride length will change with the carrying of a load such as a rucksack.
5.  Because of the angle of slope, steeper slopes have a different "real" distance to that measured on the map.
6.  Tiredness can affect the stride length.

There are a number of different courses of action that can be used to help mitigate these factors.

1. The longer the distance, the more inaccurate pace counting is. If running with a partner and there is a requirement to pace count, then split the distance between the pair, for 100 metres, the first runner pace counts the first 50 metres and the second runner the last 50 metres. This will produce an average of the two runner's stride lengths and over longer distances may prove more accurate.

2. Have a number of different pacing scales to suit different terrains and angles of slope. You'll use a different number of strides to run a hundred metres across a rough grass field than you would along a track. At the same time you would use a different number of strides for running uphill or downhill to running on the level. A small selection of different pacing scales to reflect this can help.

**Single or double pacing ?**
Paces can be counted by using either single step or a double step. Single pacing is left, right, left right and so on. Double pacing is when a single strike is used to count two paces, such as left, left, left. There is no right or wrong answer over which to chose. The important thing is to pick the style with which you feel most comfortable with.

For training exercises on pacing counting see Section 14. Training and Exercises.

**Pacing scale**
To put it simply, a pacing scale is a ruler where instead of showing distance i.e. one inch, the scale shows a number of paces i.e. twenty paces. This is then used to measure between two points and indicate the number of paces required to travel from one point to another.

In the example, right, the distance from 1 to 2 is forty paces.

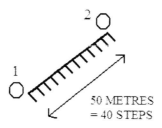

**How to make a pacing scale.**
Easy to do. If you know that it takes eighty paces to cover 100 metres
then simply mark out the length of 100 metres and then graduate it into
80ths. This can be marked onto a piece of masking tape and attached
along the edge of the compass or marked onto a laminated card/paper and
kept as a separate item.
Note that you will need different pacing scales to represent different map
scales, 1:25,000, 1:40,000 etc.

# Estimating Distance Using Time.

It is possible to estimate distance using time. Most runners have an idea of what pace they run at, for example if it takes eight minutes to run a mile then in four minutes you will do half a mile, in two minutes a quarter of a mile.

Using time to gauge distance will never be totally accurate because there are other factors that come into play such as climbing or descending or even the nature of the terrain. However, in circumstances where it is not essential to be totally accurate it can be a useful tool. For example, if your chosen route involves a stream crossing after a mile, then

1.  After six minutes running you can start looking for the stream.
2.  At around eight minutes you should expect to arrive at the stream.
3.  At ten minutes running and not having arrived at the stream, start to consider that you've gone off-course.
4.  After twelve minutes and still no stream, then you have serious problems and will need to locate and revise your course of actions.

This principle can be applied to a number of different circumstances.

## Climbing and Descending

As mentioned both in pace counting and above, problems do arrive when having to run up or down a slope due to the slowing-down and speeding-up effect.

Naismith's Rule was developed for walkers and states that for height climbed add one minute per each ten metre contour line passed. So climbing 600 metres will add sixty minutes to the time of the leg.

With some climbs you will be walking, so that this rule can be used as it is. On slopes where you can run, a variation on this rule can be developed to suit your own running pace.

The reverse applies on downhill slopes. On gentle downhill slopes of between 5% and 15% gradient then running speed will increase so that between ten and fifteen minutes can be subtracted for every 300 metres of descent.

On steeper ground above 15% gradient, then the angle is steeper and more care is needed In this case your running speed will tend to decrease. On these steep slopes then add between ten and fifteen minutes for every 300 metres of descent.

# Estimating Distance by Eye.

Some people are very good at estimating distance on the ground just by looking. They are able to see a feature and estimate it to be 100 or 200 metres away with a high degree of accuracy.

This obviously takes a great deal of practice and experience but can be done. However, as with pacing, this works best when only done over a short distance. If there is a requirement to estimate a distance of 400 metres then it would be more effective to identify a feature 100 metres away, go to it and then identify another feature a further 100 metres away, etc, etc.

The obvious drawback to this is that you are limited to line of sight. If visibility is poor or there is something blocking the view such as a clump of trees then there is little benefit from this technique.

Be aware that Naismith's Rule is a generalisation and that everybody has a different pace. It is always best to test yourself and determine your own time/pace.

# Which Technique to Use for Estimating Distance.

So which technique do you use for estimating distance ?

There is no one particular method. Most navigators will use a combination of all three as and when circumstances dictate. As a general rule of thumb, and we stress that it is general, then time is used for longer distances and pacing and/or the eyes for shorter distance. This gives you the situation where you could use all three techniques on the one leg.

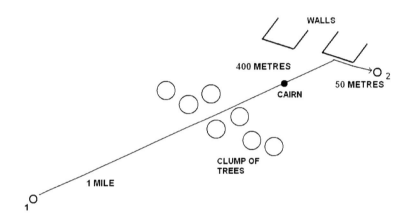

For example, the distance from point 1 to the small clump of trees is one mile and should take you roughly eight minutes. You can use an estimation of time to judge when the trees should be coming into view and when you should arrive at them.

From the trees you could estimate by eye that the cairn is 200 metres away and in line with the first set of walls. However when you make your way from the wall corner to the checkpoint at 2, pace counting the 50 metres would be the most accurate.

# 9. Techniques.

As well as the various skills that are required for navigation, there are also, as in most things, one or two techniques, that will make the task of navigation easier and more effective.

1.     Handrail technique.
2.     Catching features.
3.     Aiming-off.
4.     Running on the needle.
5.     Contouring.
6.     Steve's string.
7.     Bob's law.
8.     Stu's law.
9.     Using the other senses.

# Handrail Technique

This is a very basic technique which involves following a series of line features. The line features acting as a handrail to guide you hence the name. As we have seen previously these features are recognised easily on the map and are followed easily on the ground. However do not un-derestimate this technique. It is simple but is very effective and, if used properly, can be depended upon to get you safely from one point to an-other.

See Section 6. Map Reading for a list of line features.

Handrails are often used in navigating the first part of a leg especially to get you most of the way to an attack point. The objective should be to follow line features to as near to the control as possible. Unless you are exceptionally skilled, following a compass bearing for any great distance will not bring you out at an exact spot. The realistic alternative is to look at the map and identify features that will guide you from control to con-trol with the minimum amount of risk of losing your way.

## Examples of using the handrail technique.

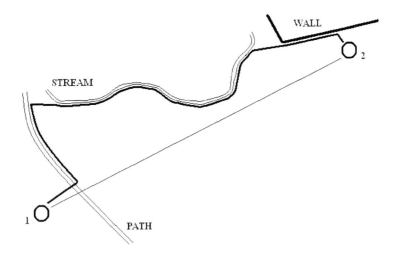

**Example 1.**

104

Using line features as a handrail to make navigation easy and reduce the risk of error.

Follow the path until the stream bend, then follow the stream until the wall. The idea is to simply join up the line features.

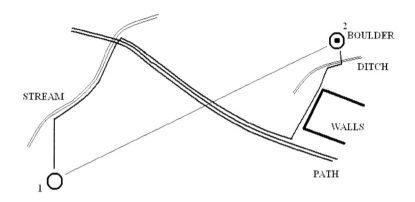

**Example 2.**

Follow the stream until you meet the path that crosses it. From there follow the path till you see the wall. At this point leave the path and follow the wall to the ditch, following the ditch should then bring you within sight of the boulder. The overall distance travelled is further than if you just went in a straight line on a bearing from 1 to 2 but there is a vastly reduced chance of missing the control.

# Catching Features

As we have seen earlier in Section 8 Advanced Skills, this technique relies on reaching a feature which will be instantly recognisable. This is called a catching feature, it catches you and prevents you from running too far.

Catching features are normally line features that are easy to recognise on the map and also on the ground. Prime examples are streams, walls, fences and paths.

Event planners try to set courses so that there are few, if any, close to a control. Fortunately it doesn't always work out that way.

The ability to identify catching features develops with experience but it is a skill that should be practiced. The ideal route should go from one catching feature to another and then lead to an attack point followed by the control.

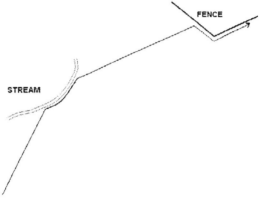

The advantages of this is that you are reducing the time-costly precise navigation to a minimum. Being able to run faster, confident that there will be features to prevent you from going wrong.

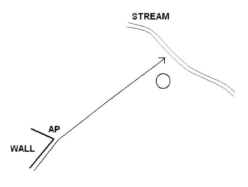

Catching features can also be used after the checkpoint to prevent you from going too far beyond the control. For example choose a stream the other side of the checkpoint. If you overshoot the checkpoint and arrive at the stream you will know not to go any further and to relocate.

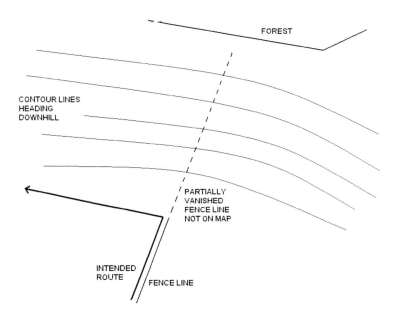

## Using contours as a catching feature

In certain circumstances and with careful use it is also possible to use contours as a catching feature. This normally applies when the angle of the ground changes, for example when changing from running on the level to running downhill or uphill.

For example the diagram above, the intended route was to follow until the end of the fence and then head off on a different heading. In reality there is a partially vanished fence line continuing on from the fence. This is not shown on the map and so it is difficult to see where the complete fence line ends. The runner mistakenly follows the partially vanished fence until they come close to reaching the forest, where they realise their mistake. By referring to the contours on the map, they should have realised that shortly after the end of the fence, the contours change from being on level ground to heading downhill. As soon as the downward slope is reached then the runner would have realised that the fence end would have been overshot.

# Aiming-Off

Following a precise bearing across country is always going to be tricky. A slight error of even half a degree can ensure that you can miss your target point. The further that you have to travel on a bearing, the further away from your target an error can take you.

One way to allow for this is to use a technique known as "aiming-off". This technique involves deliberately aiming to one side of the straight line course that you wish to follow.

## Examples of aiming-off.

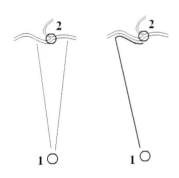

### Example 1.
When you make a bearing to a certain point, for example a stream junction, a very slight error can locate you either side of the junction. This would leave you in the situation of arriving at the stream and not knowing whether the junction was to the right or the left. By deliberately aiming-off a few degrees to the left of your bearing, in this case to end up just upstream of the junction, when you hit the stream you then know that a short distance to the right and downstream is the control.

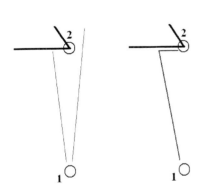

### Example 2.
Travelling on a bearing from 1 to a wall corner at 2. An error that would take you to the left of the corner would mean that you would still arrive at the wall at which point you would turn right and find the wall corner. However, if the error took you too far to the right, then you would completely miss the corner and over-shoot the control. As above, if you deliber-ately aim a few degrees to the left of your bearing then that would virtually guarantee hitting the wall from which you could then locate the corner.

# Running on the Needle.

Running on the needle is a way of saving time while using the compass. Basically it is a method of using the compass without taking the time to set it.

Remember the basics and that the red end of the compass needle always points north and that the white end always points south. In this case if you want to run due north or due south then there is no need to set the compass, simply run in the direction that either the red or white end of the needle is pointing.

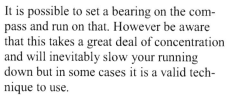

The same principle can be used to run east or west. Set the direction of travel arrow at 90 degrees to the needle and then as long as it is remaining at 90 degrees it is pointing to the east or west and you can simply follow it.

It is possible to set a bearing on the compass and run on that. However be aware that this takes a great deal of concentration and will inevitably slow your running down but in some cases it is a valid technique to use.

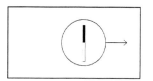
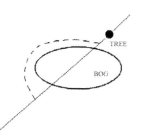

One other thing to be aware of when running on the needle is when you come to a feature that will require you to go up or down or around. In these situations it is obviously going to be difficult to maintain your original line when you come out of the change of direction.

Before you change direction, try and identify a feature on the other side of the obstacle that is on your original line of travel. When you have come out of the diversion you can then relocate to this feature before recommencing.

Running on the needle is a valid technique but does require a high degree of concentration. When ever possible look along the line of travel to identify a visible feature to head towards. It saves time and makes the task easier.

# Contouring.

One of the fundamental route choice decisions is "shall I go over or go around". Quite often the "going around" involves contouring, that is following the same height contour round the side of a hill.

Holding a constant height while keeping track of your route is notoriously difficult. It is very easy to drift down-slope and off-course. Remember, it is more natural to move down-slope than uphill or horizontal and it can often happen without any realisation of it occurring. If you happen to be fortunate enough to possess an altimeter then this task does become easier.

Contouring is usually safe when visibility is good or if you have been able to identify some catching feature which will help prevent you from straying too far off-course. The ideal checking method would be to identify some feature on the same height contour as yourself and then head towards that. This would then be repeated until the target is achieved.

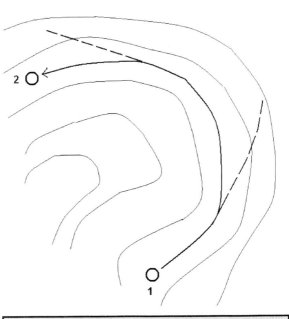

For those with one, an altimeter can be a great help when contouring.

If you can maintain a horizontal course between the contour lines then using an estimate of distance travelled would help en-

Contouring round a slope. Very easy to follow the natural inclination and drift down-slope especially as you change direction. Whenever possible try to locate some feature that is on the same contour height as you and head towards it. This may mean breaking the leg down into smaller sub-legs.

sure that your position was always known.

Contouring in the dark or with poor visibility is very difficult. The absence of any visual references means that the likelihood of drifting down-slope is very high. One way of countering this is to contour in a series of straight lines using the compass and pace counting.

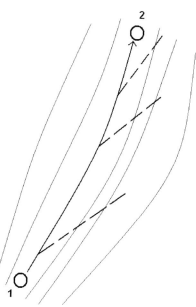

Practicing contouring in good conditions on easy, hazard-free slopes will develop the ability to contour and is well worth doing. Remember to look and identify landscape features at the same height that you can aim for.

Even when contouring relatively straight contours, it can still be easy to drift down-slope.

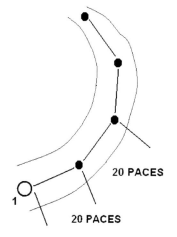

20 PACES

20 PACES

Contouring in the dark or with poor visibility. Use pace counting and a compass to contour in a series of straight lines.

111

# Steve's String.

So there you are at the start of a score event and you have a number of controls which are spread over a given area and you need to navigate to as many controls and gain as many points as possible within a set time. There is a distance v time dilemma.

A good way around this is to have a measured length of string which matches the distance that you would comfortably expect to cover within the time frame. For example, the score event may have a six hour time and you know by experience and training runs that you can cover twenty four miles within that time limit. If your map is one inch to one mile then your length of string will be twenty four inches. On your map you can then lay out your string and use it to plan your route and the various controls that you will visit.

When there is a second day of competition then generally the time allowed will be less than the first day, so make a mark on your string relative to the second day's time limit and repeat the process.

To save on weight use your string as a lanyard for your compass.

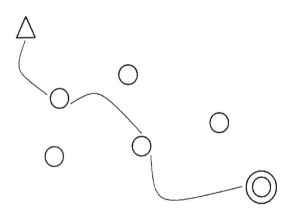

# Bob's Law.

When we come onto route choice in the next section, one of the fundamental decisions is "do I go left or do I go right". The answer to this is to compare the relative distances involved in the two courses of action. Obviously the shorter distance wins and, all other things being equal, that is the route you should take.

Bob's law is a relatively simple and easy method of comparing the distance of a specific route to that of a straight-line route. Be aware that it is not particularly accurate but it is easy to use and in most cases it will indicate the route that is the shorter.

The law is based on one of the rules of geometry and states that in the diagram below, the furthest distance that route A is from route B is the amount that route A is longer than route B.

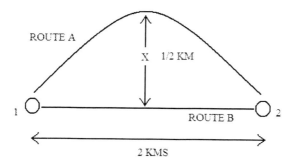

In the diagram the maximum distance between route A and route B is X = 0.5 kms long.

So how is this used practically.

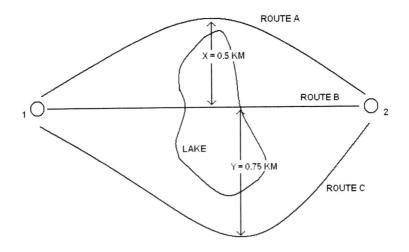

In the situation above, there is a choice of either going left, route A, or right, route C, around a lake. Draw the straight line route in on your map, route B. If the furthest distance route A is from route B is 0.5 km and route B is 2 km then the total distance of route A is 2.5 km.

Using the same logic, if the furthest distance of route C from route B is 0.75 km and route B is 2 km then the total distance of route C is 2.75 km.
Route A= 2.5 km
Route C= 2.75 km

Then route A is the shorter and should be followed.

Remember that this technique is not totally accurate but as a quick and easy estimator it does work.

In describing both the Bob's Law and the Stu's Law techniques no mention is made of terrain or other factors. Both of these techniques just estimate relevant distance and as this section progresses you will see that other factors can and will influence your route choice decisions as well as the relative distance involved.

# Stu's Law.

As we'll see in Section 10 Route Choice, one of the fundamental route choice decisions is to go up or around, do you go over the hill or around it. The decision should be based on the relative distance of the two routes. The choice being to take the shorter distance.

This then poses the question of how do you judge the relative distance of the two routes when one will obviously include a lot more climbing than the other.

One method is to assume that the vertical distance climbed is equivalent to running a set distance on level ground. Normally it is found that 100 metres of vertical climb is the equivalent of running one kilometre on the level.

It is now possible to count the number of contour lines to arrive at the additional distance travelled through climbing.

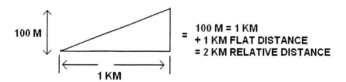

Counting individual contour lines can be a little bit awkward/difficult while actually navigating for real in the field. As we saw in Section 5 Map Reading, OS maps use a prominent thicker line on every fifth contour line called the index contour. It is far easier to count the index contours than each individual line. Bearing in mind that each index contour represents 50 metres height gain then the number of index counted would have to be multiplied by 0.5 to give the equivalent in 100's of metres, i.e. four index contours counted x 0.5 = 200 metres climbed.

This principle can now be applied to the following example.

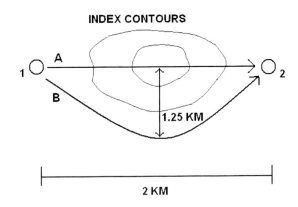

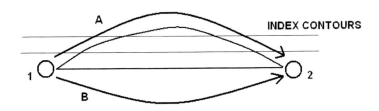

Route A = 2 index contours x 0.5 = 100 metres = 1 km of flat running +
2 km of flat running = 3 kms in total.
Or ( 2 x 0.5 ) + 2 = 3 kms

Route B = 2 km of flat running + 1.25 km (see Bob's Law) = 3.25 km in
total.

Route A has the shorter relative distance.

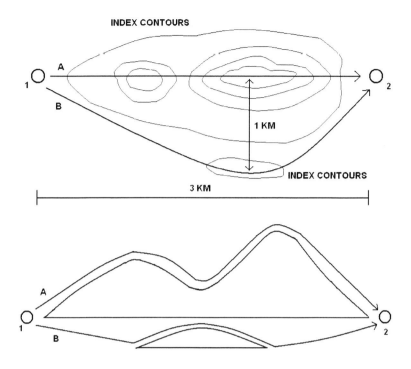

Route A = (3 + 3) index contours x 0.5 + 3 km = 6 km.

Route B = 1 index contour x 0.5 + (3 km + 1 km) = 4.5 km.

Route B has the shorter relative distance.

As can be seen this rule works for the 50 metre index contours that are found on OS maps. With Harvey's maps the index contour uses a 75 metre interval. In this case if you substitute 0.75 for the 0.5 used is the formulae then it will still work.

Number of index contours x 0.75 + distance on flat.

The formulae can now be stated as :

Number of index contours x decimal of height index + flat ground distance = relative distance.

Remember that this technique is not totally accurate but as a quick and easy estimator it does work.

# Using the Other Senses

With the best will in the world, navigating in very poor visibility can be tricky. Even fine navigation may only get you within a couple of feet of the control. So what other tricks are there that may help.

Obviously poor visibility affects the sense of sight but don't forget that you have other senses and if you think about using them, they can actually help you zero in on your target once you have got close to the control.

Firstly, use your hearing. The conditions that produce poor visibility such as low cloud or mist can quite often produce a stillness that can seem to magnify sound. Noises that you wouldn't give much regard to in good weather can take on a whole new meaning when the clag is down. Obviously with high wind and poor visibility you're still going to be stuck but sometimes even a mild wind can be helpful in creating a noise when everything else is silent.

Examples of using your ears:
1. Listening for the sound of running water when you need to approach a stream.
2. Listening for the sound of rustling trees when approaching a coppice surrounded by open moorland.

Secondly, using the sense of feeling. Examples of using the sense of feeling include:
1. The wind on your face, when you get closer to the more exposed summit tops or cliff sides the wind speed will increase and you will feel the effects against your body.
2. The texture of the ground underfoot, when you are expecting to traverse a marshy or boggy area you will feel the transformation from hard to soft ground under your feet.
3. The change of gradient, on gradual gradients it may be difficult to tell visually when the angle of slope changes and whether you are ascending or descending  but the feeling in your legs and feet will indicate this change.

Feeling and hearing are techniques gathered from experience, from being out in the hills and should not be used as a definitive skill that can give a yes/no decision on a direction although they can help in arriving at that decision. However, you can have some fun trying out these powers of observation.

# 10. Route choice.

What is route choice.
Route choice is quite simply deciding which way to go from one point to another.

When is route choice done.
For the runner running in the outdoors, exercising route choice can be done in a number of different circumstances.

1.      At home deciding which way your training run is going to go.
2.      During an actual run when circumstances dictate that you have to change your proposed route. This may be due to weather conditions or quite simply the route being harder than expected and you find that you are running out of time to complete.
3.      During competition when your navigational ability is being tested and you have to decide your route from one point to another.

In all these circumstances the basic principles of route choice remain the same. There is no real difference in technique between sitting at home deciding tomorrow's training run and being out on the hill in a mountain marathon and choosing your route from checkpoint 5 to 6. The methods employed are basically the same. The obvious big difference is that one is done in a relaxed environment while the other is the heat of competition. However, this does mean that you can practise your competitive route finding in the comfort of your own home.

For runners the aim of route choice is to choose a route that will give you the overall fastest running speed and thus the shortest time on course.

# The Basic Route Choice Decisions.

There are some simple route choice rules. However, bear in mind that there are no simple right or wrong answers, the principal behind route choice is to choose the route that will give you the least overall travelling time. In some circumstances one option will give you the fastest time, in other circumstances it will be the other option. The trick is to look at every leg with an open mind and form a judgment.

Route choice decisions are based on
1.      Up or around,
2.      Left or right,
3.      Up or down,
4.      Good or bad terrain, and
5.      Path or no path.

## Up or around
Quite simply, do you go up and over the hill or do you go around. The basic decision is based on volume of effort required normally expressed as relative distance.
For method of judging relative distance see Stu's law in Section 9 Techniques.

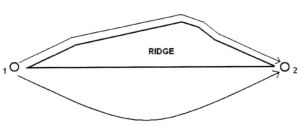

## Left or right
This decision is do you go to the left or right of an object. This will depend upon the relative distances involved. An indicator of the relevant distances would be obtained by using Bob's Law.

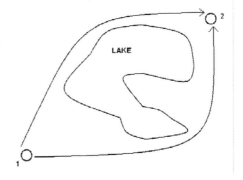

### Up or down
A similar sort of decision as
the up or around question. In
this case is it up and around the
valley or down and up the
other side.

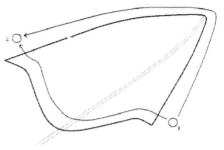

### Good or bad terrain
Do you take a shorter route
over bad terrain or take a
longer route over terrain that is
more suitable to running.

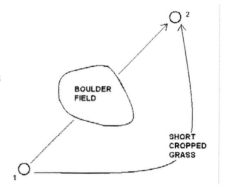

### Path or no path
Do you take a longer route on
a navigationally easy and
more runnable path or take a
more risky route across country.

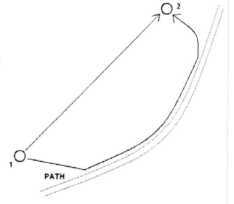

These are the basic decisions but as always nothing is as simple as all that. Legs in competition maybe a couple of miles long. Therefore the route choice may involve all of these decisions or any combination. This will involve breaking a leg down into sections, see later in this section.

In order to make the best route choice you need to rely on your own experience and be confident enough to trust in your own ability. This comes from practise and knowledge of your own abilities.

# Factors that Influence Decision Making.

We've looked at the basic route choice decisions but with every decision you have to choose one way or another. This means that there has to be a factor that influences your choice. This can depend upon your fitness, your mental agility, even how far into an event you are. Below is a list of most of the possible factors that can help you make your decisions.

1.    How fast can you run over different types of terrain.
2.    Do you have the strength to run as fast over rough terrain as you can on a path.
3.    Do you have the experience and confidence to run fast over open country away from line and hand rail features.
4.    How far are you prepared to run round instead of going over.
5.    Do you navigate more slowly when you are away from the relative safety of paths.
6.    How far into the event is it, if it is the early stages do you play it safe.
7.    Are you feeling tired, physically and/or mentally.
8.    Are you starting to have lapses in concentration.
9.    Have you just made a mistake on a leg.
10.   Will the control be more visible by going up and over and then looking down onto it.
11.   Are there more recognisable features to help guide you on one route choice than on another.

---

**Rest Breaks**
When calculating the time to be taken for each of your route legs, always allow a five minute break in every hour. This will allow a bit of recovery and the chance to re-hydrate and refresh. Plan this properly at the right location such as a stream crossing and it will allow you to replenish your fluid stocks. On a day where you are going to be out for six to eight hours, planned stops are more effective and time saving than pushing on and having enforced stops through fatigue.

---

# Foreshortening Effect.

A  map is a flat representation of the landscape. This in itself can give problems in route choice and to a limited degree in navigation. Imagine looking down from a plane and seeing a cliff, the cliff will look similar to a single line or a narrow band. In reality it may be 1,000 feet high.

This is known as the foreshortening effect and relates to the "hidden" extra distance created by the angle of slope.

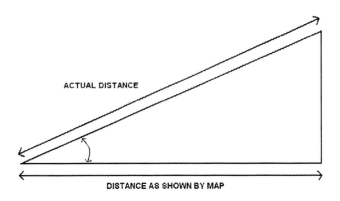

Actual distance is longer than the horizontal distance as shown on the map. Steep slopes appear to be shorter than they actually are.

Under normal circumstances this effect is relatively insignificant and can be discounted. However when it comes to steeper slopes the actual distance along the ground can be substantially greater than that of the horizontal distance shown by the map.

The steeper the slope the more significant the effect. On a slope of 30 degrees the extra distance involved is 15%, for every 100 metres on the map you physically travel 115 metres. On a 45 degree slope the physical distance becomes closer to 140 metres.

The table below gives the approximate additional distance travelled compared to the horizontal distance.

| Slope angle in degrees | Additional distance |
| --- | --- |
| 10 | 1.5% |
| 20 | 6% |
| 30 | 15% |
| 40 | 31% |
| 45 | 41% |
| 50 | 56% |
| 60 | 100% |

As can be seen any route choice that involves steep angles of slope needs to have the foreshortening effect factored in. If using variations of formulae such as Naismith's Rule to work out an estimation of time taken then you will find that they will include an adjustment for foreshortening. However if you are just using your own rule of thumb then you will need to factor-in some adjustment particularly in an area of long steep hills.

# Recognising Ground and Terrain Types and How They Affect Route Decisions.

Difficult terrain can drastically reduce your running speed. Bog, snow, high vegetation and boulder fields can slow your pace by as much as 80% if you are forced to walk. In order to choose your best route you need to be able to identify the nature of the terrain from the information contained on the map some of which may not be that obvious.

Terrain also poses a challenge to the body. See our sister publication, Terrain Training for Off-Road Runners, for advice on how to run across different types of terrain more effectively.

## Recognising Terrain and Ground Type.

Harvey's maps are ones normally used for events such as mountain marathons. They provide a great deal more information on the nature of the terrain than OS.

The land type is split into the following categories.

1. Improved pasture shown as dark yellow. Grazing areas for live stock. Usually good running terrain but often marked as out of bounds areas on events.
2. Rough pasture. Shown as pale yellow. Again another area where live stock are grazed. Capable of being run over at a fairly good speed but more care will be needed than on improved pasture as the ground will be more uneven and rougher.
3. Fell or Moorland. Shown as white. The type of terrain that the majority of the event will be held over. The ground can be a mixture of different types.
4. Open forest or woodland. Shown as pale green. Well spaced-out plantations of trees that will probably allow fairly good running.
5. Dense plantation. Shown as dark green. Closely packed plantations of trees. Usually virtually impossible to run in and often quite difficult to walk through. Best avoided like the plague unless you can identify a suitable path or forest ride to follow.
6. New plantation. Shown as green dots on a white background. As the name suggests a new planting of immature trees. Bear in mind that at the initial planting the young trees are quite densely packed and over the years they are thinned out. As a result the running is not normally that good.

As well as the different colourations it is possible to gain knowledge of the running conditions from other information on the map such as contour lines and certain point and line features.

## Ridge

Shown by the contour lines rising closely-grouped together to meet on either side of a flatter area. This indicates a fairly level ridge. Ridges are normally relatively dry areas as water drains-off to either side. This usually makes them a good, fast running surface, however, see the note on boggy ground below. Be aware that ridges can get quite narrow and the narrower the ridge, the greater the possibility of a broken, rocky surface. This in turn means a slow running speed. With ridges there is always going to be an element of climbing to get up to the ridge. This gives the question of is the additional climbing going to be worth the increased running speed.

## Valley

The contours form a vague "V" such as the Langdale valley in the Lakes or "U" shape such as High Cup in the North Pennines. Normally formed by the erosion effects of water over time. Most valleys have a water course of one type or another along their floor. Lower down the valley ground conditions tend to be dryer while higher up where the head-waters tend to converge the ground will be wetter and more criss-crossed by streams. Small valleys may also be quite narrow and steep-sided, not allowing much room to run.

## Boggy ground

Plan to avoid bogs. Both the OS and Harvey's maps have symbols for bogs and marshes. Harvey's are good on this aspect as they define the boundaries of the bog. Also consider the types of terrain that will hold water and be boggy. Likely spots will include valley and corrie floors near water courses, broad cols, hollows on light ridges and plateaus, reservoir and tarn/loch margins, moorland and areas around springs and stream heads. The vegetation gives more clues. Course grass, cotton grass, sphagnum moss and myrtle abound in wet ground. Keep your eyes open for any lush vegetation, it is a good clue to the ground conditions. Place names can also be used. If the ridge has the word "moss" in it's name then you can guarantee that it's not because of it's desert– like conditions. The term "head" normally means the beginning of one or several watercourses so again expect wet and boggy conditions.

## Grouse butts

The showing of grouse butts on the maps is an obvious indicator that the area is used for grouse shooting. Grouse feed on heather therefore expect a heather moorland with a minimum of ankle deep heather and a poor running surface. In the early part of the year when heather burning has produced bare sections and the resulting young growth, then the running may be slightly better in these sections. In the main, stick to tracks and paths when crossing heather.

## Walls

Walls tend to be built on dryer ground than fence lines. The dry ground supports the weight of the wall whereas the lighter fence post line will cross more marshy ground that a wall can't. In addition to this a wall provides more shade which means that vegetation does not tend to grow right up close to the wall. Normally there is a small space alongside the wall which can provide reasonable running while the ground just a few feet away can be totally different. Fence lines don't have the same characteristics.

## Forest rides

One of the problems with running in woods and forests is the terrain. Tracks and paths are fine and would normally give good running. Unfortunately you also have what are called forest rides, also sometimes known as firebreaks. These are deliberate gaps between blocks of forest planting. On maps these are often shown as a line of white space which insinuates that the ride is similar to a forest road or track which is also shown as a white space but with a dotted line on either side. This is made even more confusing as often the ride can be a continuation of a road or track that has ended.

These rides may exist on the ground, sometimes with a path along them. Unfortunately in a lot of cases they don't and it is quite common to plan a route following a ride only to be met by a wall of greenery that, being realistic, is quite impenetrable.

Care should always be taken when using forest rides. Without prior knowledge it can be very uncertain what type of ground conditions you will meet.

## Peat hags

These can be found in most parts of upland UK but are notorious in the Peak District. With their soft ground underfoot and constant up and down movement, travelling over this type of terrain seriously drains energy reserves and slows you down. Navigationally, it is also difficult as many features such as summits and cairns become difficult to see. This type of terrain is identified on Harvey's maps but not on OS which, unless you have local knowledge, makes them difficult to identify. Unless you have no choice, always try to avoid areas of peat hags.

## Sheep trods
Paths through vegetation caused by repeated passage of sheep. Not shown on maps although specialist orienteering maps may show them as paths.

Very handy to use if they are going in the required direction. Can allow faster paced running than beating your way through the heather. However be aware that just as sheep meander so do sheep trods. Don't blindly follow them, they may change direction and take you away from your targeted route. As you use them keep monitoring the direction of travel to ensure that it is still going the way that you want.

# Breaking a Leg Down into Sections.

There is the old joke about how do you eat an elephant. The answer - one mouthful at a time. This same principle also applies to navigation. On most events the distance between controls or checkpoints may be several miles especially in mountain marathons. Navigating distances like this can be difficult and because distance can magnify errors, one small mistake can result in being a substantial distance away from the control at the end of the leg.

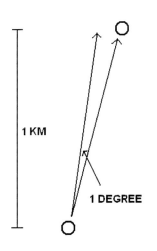

Legs should be broke down into smaller sections and the navigation on each section should be kept as simple as possible. Follow the KISS principle - Keep It Simple Stupid !!

Look along the length of the leg and identify intermediate targets to aim for on the way to the control. Also assess which areas are going to give you problems and which areas are going to be easy navigation. Don't always assume that fine navigation will only be used on the final stretch from the attack point to the control. There may be a stretch part-way through the leg that presents navigational difficulties and will require more care.

Identify features, sections of quiet and busy ground and things to avoid such as crags and marshy ground. This will help make suitable route choices.

**Busy ground** is an area that is rich in features and so can be complex and difficult to navigate over.
**Quiet ground** is the opposite where an area is relatively featureless.

A typical leg may look like.

LEG 3  –

Section 1  -  using the stream as a handrail to stream bend A.

Section 2  -  running on the needle to the large re-entrant at B.

Section 3  -  rough navigation to the wall at C and then follow the wall to the attack point at AP.

Section 4  -  using fine navigation and compass work from the attack point to the control 2.

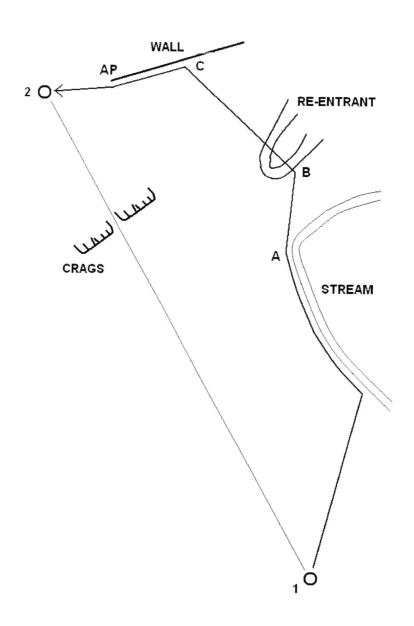

WALL

AP

C

2

RE-ENTRANT

B

CRAGS

A

STREAM

1

# Gauging Stream Widths.

At some point the route decision you make will involve crossing a stream, a beck, a burn or whatever you want to call it. Now it will come in handy if you know before hand whether the stream will be jumpable or whether you will need to wade across. Obviously as well as the time element involved there is also the safety aspect particularly in times of bad weather when streams will be running higher than normal.

It is possible to estimate the width of a stream from looking at the map. While not totally accurate due to the effects of scale, generally the thicker the blue line representing the stream then the wider the stream.

On the following maps. The following is a rough guide.

**OS 1:50,000**

| | | |
|---|---|---|
| Single thin blue line | - | less than 4 metres wide. |
| Single thick blue line | - | between 4 to 8 metres wide. |
| Two blue lines coloured between | - | wider than 8 metres. |

**OS 1:25,000**

| | | |
|---|---|---|
| Single blue line | - | up to 4 metres. |
| Two blue lines coloured between | - | over 4 metres. |

**Harvey's 1:40,000**
Similar to OS 1:50,000

When planning your route always consider the stream crossings and the effects of the weather. Even relatively moderate rainfalls can make stream crossings a lot more difficult and risky. Bear in mind that it does- n't have to be an injury or near-drowning to cause withdrawal from an event. A good dunking can saturate your kit, cause damage to the kit or even result in the loss of some or all of it.

Also even if it is a fine sunny day, consider what the weather has been like over the preceding couple of days. Sometimes rain can take it's time to work it's effect on streams and quite often they are still running quite high a day or so after the rain has stopped.

In the example below, during normal weather conditions it may be per- fectly acceptable to take a straight line course from 1 to 2, crossing the stream at C1 where, although you may get your feet wet, the crossing would be relatively safe and secure. In periods where rainfall has oc-

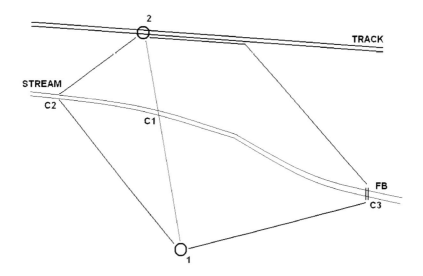

curred then it may be a bit more prudent to head further upstream to C2 where the stream may be narrower and the crossing less risky. In severe weather you can have the situation where no matter how far upstream you go, the depth and speed of the water will not allow a risk-free crossing. In this situation, you may just have to bite the bullet and accept that you would have to travel some distance to find a bridge further downstream, C3.

Stream crossings always have the potential to be dangerous both to you and your kit. Never assume that you will be able to cross without incident, you may be in for a shock. Check the map to estimate it's width and consider both the current and the previous couple of days weather conditions.

# The Effects of Weather on Route Choice.

Weather conditions can have an effect on your choice of route forcing you to choose a route that is not the optimum but which may be the best of a poor choice.

Weather conditions will affect your route choice through the following ways.

1.  It may effect your ability to navigate and put you in the position where the risk of navigational errors is increased.
2.  It may affect your own personal safety and put you in a position of unacceptable risk.
3.  It may effect your ability to run and lead to increased leg times.

**Example.**
If the wind is gale force and is coming from the west and you are travelling from East to West, do you

1.  go up on to a high ridge into the wind following the shorter, direct route, or
2.  stay low and contour round the ridge.

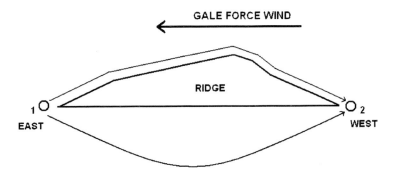

Depending upon the circumstances and the relevant extra distances involved, based on either Stu or Bob's law, you would decide to go around or over. However, because of the debilitating effect of the wind, the general rule would be to stay low.

The weather will affect you in the following ways:

**Wind**
A strong head wind can significantly slow down your running speed.

134

Also never under-estimate the effect of running against a strong wind can have on your energy reserves. After a long day fighting against the wind, you can end up being very seriously fatigued. Strong winds can also pre sent a safety issue with the danger of being blown-over or hit by flying objects. As a general rule try and avoid any routes that would leave you exposed to strong winds unless you judge that there would be a signifi-cant advantage in following one of these routes. The optimum route in these circumstances would normally be low lying and sheltered.

## Rain

Rain can affect you in four ways

1. You will get cold and wet. This can present safety issues through possible hypothermia.
2. Spending long periods out in the cold and wet can affect your abil-ity to concentrate leading to navigation mistakes.
3. Any weather conditions that will involve running with a hood up will make communication with your partner difficult and can make you feel isolated and have a detrimental effect on morale.
4. Rain affects the nature of ground causing mud and wet clingy vegetation. Both of these can slow down your running speed.
5. Rain can cause swollen rivers and streams. These can present problems to running speed and also safety concerns when crossing them.

Again, as a general rule, in times of heavy rain, avoid the more exposed routes and choose the more sheltered. Try and choose the more naviga-tionally safer options, such as following line features and using hand rails.

## Snow and Ice

Snow and ice have similar effects as rain but only more severe plus the obvious safety issues concerning foot plant and slipping. In addition there is the increased likelihood of navigational error due to land features being hidden and obscured by the snow. There is also the possibility of poor visibility through white-outs and spin-drift. If possible avoid entering the snowline and stay on the more sheltered low level routes. Often, depend-ant upon the snow fall, this is not possible. In this cause try to keep to the sheltered routes where the risk of drifts is lower.

## Thunderstorms

It is not a good time to be in open land or mountain tops when there is a thunderstorm about. The threat of a lightning strike is increased. In this case stick to routes that are low-lying and sheltered.

**Fog and Mist**
Both these obscure your visibility and make navigation more difficult, increasing the risk of error. In the case of cloud inversions try and get above the mist level and into clear sky. For more details on navigating in the dark and poor visibility see Section 12 .

**Heat**
Heat can cause discomfort and dehydration. This can effect your concentration causing navigation errors. At its worst it can affect safety through heat exhaustion and heat stroke. Ensure that you stay well hydrated. If not carrying enough fluid this may involve plotting your chosen route in order to find streams from which to drink. Consider planning routes that involve running at a height such as over a ridge. This may result in cooler conditions and more comfortable running hence a faster time although there may be less opportunity to pick up fluid.

**Escape Routes**
In times of bad weather, there is always the temptation to risk a more exposed route in order to save a little bit of time. At the end of the day this all boils down to route choice and the decisions that you make. However it is always advisable to have an escape route planned in case the weather conditions turn out to be worse than anticipated.

An escape route is an alternative route that allows you to abandon the original route and relocate to a safer course. For example in the situation below an escape route would be a path that would allow you to leave the exposed high-level ridge route and descend to the more sheltered low-level route.

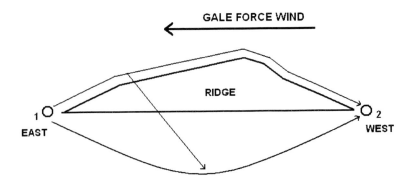

# 11. Controls.

Controls are always placed on an identifiable feature. This feature may be either a

1. Line feature,
2. Contour feature,
3. Point feature, or a
4. Spot height.

## Line feature.

As we have discussed before in Section 6. Map Reading, line features are features that form a line across the map such as roads. Tracks, paths, walls, fences, rivers, streams and ditches. Controls can be placed at specific points along these features. Normally these would be such as Junctions, corners and bends. Usually controls on line features are relatively easy to locate because the line feature itself can be used as a handrail. However care does need to be taken if the control is placed at the end of a line feature.

## Contour feature.

Again as shown in Section 6, contours are lines that represent the shape of the ground. Points where the shape of the land changes can be used as control sites. Examples of these would be re-entrants, knolls, gullies, spurs, summits, ridges and cols. Controls on contour features are normally best approached from above. They are more visible when looking down in them than when trying to see them from below.

## Point feature.

Unless they are very close to a path, point features are harder to find than line features or contour features. When point features are used for controls, then the kite is normally hung on the side of the feature that is furthest from the obvious direction of approach. This means that the feature is located before the kite.

Read the description sheet carefully. If it says something like "Boulder, South Side" and you approach from the north then you will see the boulder before the kite. In this case it would be best to overshoot the control and see the kite rather than stop short in front of the boulder.

As a rule, point features make harder control sites. Sunken point features such as depressions and pits are harder than raised point features and require considerable concentration to locate.

## Spot heights.

On the maps where there is no distinctive height features. You may find what is called a "spot height". This is where in the absence of a distinctive summit, the marker has indicated the height of a particular point in order to provide a reference. This spot height may or may not be the highest spot in

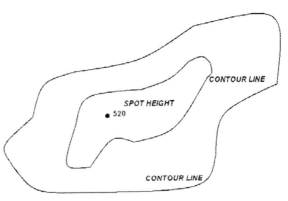

the surrounding area. As with contour lines themselves, the dot that marks the spot height and the numbers of the height are printed in brown.

These spot heights can sometimes be used as controls by the course planner. As such there does tend to be nothing physically there other than the control kite and dibber/punch. These type of controls normally require pin-point navigation from a close-at-hand attack point.

A variation on the spot height control is where a line, contour or point feature is combined with a height. Examples of this would include a fence line going uphill and control being at a point where it crosses a specific contour line.

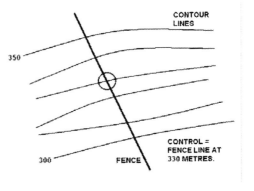

Certain types of control have their own peculiarities and require particular care. If the control is in an area of low visibility due to high bracken/other vegetation or on a steep slope then approach the control on a level route rather than diagonally up or down the slope. Sunken features are less visible and care needs to be taken. Point features need more care than line or contour features.

The majority of control sites have a direction of approach that will make them the most visible. This may mean approaching them from above, from the same level or from below. In the example below the control is at its most visible when being looked down on. So if possible pick an attack-point that is up-slope of the control and descend down towards it.

Controls located mid-way up a slope can be difficult to see from below. If possible always try and plan a route that enables you to approach them from above.

The list of control features is endless so never underestimate the ingenuity of the course planner. However the following matrix identifies the most common and illustrates what they are, what they look like and how to approach them.

| Control location | Path junction |
|---|---|
| What it is | Junction where one path joins another, paths may not be very distinct |
| What it physically looks like |  |
| Best approached from | Using one of the paths as a line feature |

| Control location | Path bend |
|---|---|
| What it is | Bend in a path |
| What it physically looks like |  |
| Best approached from | Using the path as a line feature |

| Control location | Stream bend |
|---|---|
| What it is | Bend in a stream, the bend may not be that pronounced |
| What it physically looks like |  |
| Best approached from | Using the stream as a line feature |

| Control location | Stream source |
|---|---|
| What it is | Source of a spring where it issues from the ground, often in re-entrant |
| What it physically looks like |  |
| Best approached from | Using the stream as a line feature |

| Control location | Stream junction |
|---|---|
| What it is | Junction where one stream joins another, streams may not be that wide |
| What it physically looks like |  |
| Best approached from | Using one of the streams as a line feature |

| Control location | Fence corner |
|---|---|
| What it is | Corner in a fence line |
| What it physically looks like |  |
| Best approached from | Using the fence as a line feature |

| Control location | Wall corner |
| --- | --- |
| What it is | Corner in a wall line. Normally an outside corner but sometimes may be an inside corner which may be more difficult to see. |
| What it physically looks like |  |
| Best approached from | Using the wall as a line feature |

| Control location | Waterfall |
| --- | --- |
| What it is | Either one or a series of drops in a watercourse. |
| What it physically looks like |  |
| Best approached from | Using the water course as a line feature |

| Control location | Re-entrant |
| --- | --- |
| What it is | Shallow valley maybe only one or two contour lines high. |
| What it physically looks like |  |
| Best approached from | From above. |

| Control location | Knoll |
| --- | --- |
| What it is | Small raised hill, maybe only one or two contour lines high but may be attached as an offshoot to a main hill feature. |
| What it physically looks like |  |
| Best approached from | From the side or parallel to the contour lines. |

| Control location | Gully |
|---|---|
| What it is | Normally a sunken course of a stream which may still flow or be dry. |
| What it physically looks like | |
| Best approached from | If possible using the gully as a line feature |

| Control location | Depression |
|---|---|
| What it is | A shallow pit, often the result of some industrial activity but may be natural. |
| What it physically looks like | |
| Best approached from | As a sunken point feature, depressions are normally difficult to locate. Best approached slowly from a relatively close attack point, if possible, from above or sideways. |

| | |
|---|---|
| Control location | Spur |
| What it is | A small, short ridge, the control may be at foot or on top |
| What it physically looks like | |
| Best approached from | If possible from above |

| | |
|---|---|
| Control location | Crag |
| What it is | Small crag not normally much bigger than head height |
| What it physically looks like | |
| Best approached from | Below or if possible using a line of crags as line feature |

| | |
|---|---|
| Control location | Crag foot |
| What it is | The foot of a larger crag |
| What it physically looks like |  |
| Best approached from | Below or if possible using a line of crags as a line feature |

| | |
|---|---|
| Control location | Large boulder, |
| What it is | A large individual stone. If part of a group, fine navigation may be required to locate individual boulder. |
| What it physically looks like |  |
| Best approached from | On a compass bearing unless another feature can be used to point you in the correct direction. |

| | |
|---|---|
| Control location | Small boulder |
| What it is | Smaller than a large boulder but still a large individual stone. If part of a group, fine navigation may be required to locate individual boulder. |
| What it physically looks like |  |
| Best approached from | On a compass bearing unless another feature can be used to point you in the correct direction. |

| | |
|---|---|
| Control location | Summit |
| What it is | The top of a peak, the highest point. |
| What it physically looks like |  |
| Best approached from | If possible along a ridgeline but it is always going to be from below. |

| | |
|---|---|
| Control location | Ridge |
| What it is | Long, narrow strip often leading away from a summit. |
| What it physically looks like |  |
| Best approached from | From above or the base of the ridge. |

| | |
|---|---|
| Control location | Col |
| What it is | The lowest point between two joined hills. |
| What it physically looks like |  |
| Best approached from | From above or from below the col. |

| | |
|---|---|
| Control location | Lochan , tarn, pool. |
| What it is | A pool of water often at a high elevation. Normally the control sheet will specify a particular side of the pool such as "north west side". |
| What it physically looks like |  |
| Best approached from | From above. |

| | |
|---|---|
| Control location | Marsh edge |
| What it is | An area of soft, boggy ground. Will vary in size and degree of softness quite often with the time of year and weather conditions. Normally the control sheet will specify a particular side of the marsh. |
| What it physically looks like |  |
| Best approached from | From the dry edge direction as opposed to crossing the marsh. |

| | |
|---|---|
| Control location | Forest edge |
| What it is | The edge line of a change in vegetation from field or moor to a wooded area. There may or may not be a wall or fence boundary along the edge of the forest. |
| What it physically looks like |  |
| Best approached from | From a facing or 90 degrees to the edge direction. |

# 12. Navigating in Darkness and Poor Visibility.

Navigating in clear weather conditions is great but in a country such as ours, even in summer, there is no guarantee of those perfect conditions. In darkness or thick mist even the most familiar landscape can become disorientating.

The first thing to learn about navigating in darkness and poor visibility is that there are no special techniques for when you cannot see. All the techniques that you have been shown and have learnt previously in this book still apply. The one big difference is how you use them and the degree of concentration that is required.

The main problem in navigating with poor visibility is self-doubt. When you can't fully see the ground features that you are moving through, then it becomes very easy to question what you are doing. Clear conditions provide reassurance when you can move past tick-off features fairly easily. This is obviously not the case when the struggle is to see those self-same tick-off features and self-doubt can creep in. The answer to this is to remain positive about the decisions and actions you have taken. Don't go changing your plan unless there is clear evidence that you have gone wrong.

Precision is a lot more important with poor visibility. Because a checkpoint is less visible you will need to get a lot closer to it before you can see it. Unlike in daylight you can't rely on seeing it from a distance. This lack of visibility also makes travelling on a bearing more difficult. The tried and trusted technique of sighting on a fixed point in the distance wouldn't work because you just can't see that far ahead. This is where the technique of leapfrogging becomes extremely useful. Leapfrogging is where you use your partner as the fixed point. See Section 7 Fundamental Skills.

Not being able to see gives a much greater chance of error. Even normally simple moves become much more difficult in the dark or low cloud. You need to go back to basics and follow the KISS principle and keep everything simple. Use handrails as much as possible. If there is a longer route that makes navigation simpler this might be worth following, in the longer term it may save time.

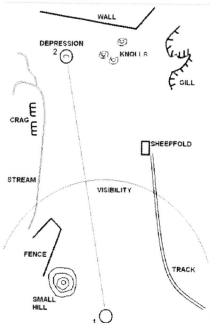

In dark or poor visibility things can start to look different, distances can become exaggerated and it becomes a lot easier to drift off-course especially if travelling across slopes or through difficult vegetation. Under normal conditions you can use your eyes to fix a point in the distance and navigate towards that make any route corrections or deviations as you go. This can't be done in poor visibility as the distance suddenly becomes a lot nearer. It then becomes necessary to slow things down and navigate from feature to feature. Effectively breaking the leg down into smaller chunks.

It is stating the obvious but with good visibility the distance that you can see is far greater than when visibility is poorer. This gives you the ability to use rough navigation with confidence as there are a large number of tick-off features available to use in order to monitor your progress and ensure that you are keeping on course.

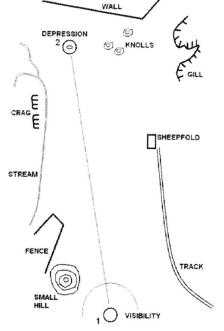

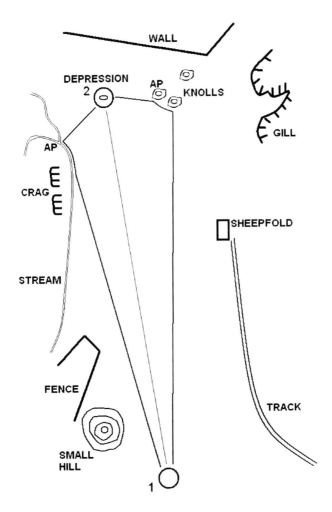

As you can see good visibility will allow you to run less precisely. Using the left route choice you can head towards the stream to use the stream junction as the attack point. On the way you will be able to use the small hill, the fence line and the crags as tick-off features to ensure that you were moving on the correct heading and to monitor your rough position.

The same would apply if you chose to use the right hand route choice. In this case you would use the track, sheepfold, gill mouth and knolls as the tick-off features.

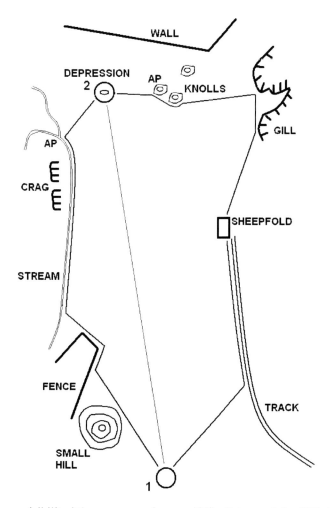

In poorer visibility it becomes much more difficult to use tick-off features because you just quite simply can't see them. In this case you have to break the leg down into shorter sections with easily recognisable and lo-catable targets and at the same time slow the running pace down so that they cannot be easily over-shot or missed.

In the example, on the left leg a bearing would be taken on the fence line. The upward slope of the small hill on the left would help check the course direction. The fence line would be followed until the corner was reached where you could then head off to the stream. The using the stream as a handrail would lead you to the attack point at the junction. Notice that this variation of the left hand route is longer than the one used in daylight utilising rough navigation. But by staying in closer contact with the tick-off features and using handrail techniques as much as possible, the risk of any navigational errors is much reduced.

The same principles would apply if you chose the right hand leg. You would travel further to the right to make contact with the track which you would then use as a handrail to the sheepfold.

On events held later in the year when the dark nights start cutting in, such as on the OMM, with a long day out there is always the possibility of finishing the last leg or legs in twilight or semi-darkness. Familiarity of and being prepared for navigating in the dark will ensure a successful completion of the course.

# Scenarios

Below are a couple of scenarios where the runner can be caught out by poor visibility and darkness.

## Lost on a Mountain in Mist.

Actions.
1.   Stop.
2.   Think.
3.   Keep an open mind.
4.   Look around you.
5.   Take an aspect of slope (estimating slope angle).

Even with mist it should be possible to tell which direction is downhill. With an aspect of slope you should be able to find a corresponding slope on the map in the rough vicinity of where you think that you are.
If there are no obvious dangers and it is safe to do so, systematically move up and down the slope to try and locate a collecting feature such as a wall or a stream. Something that will help confirm your position.
Once your position has been fixed, plan a route to safety. Utilise short legs on the route and try to identify as many features as possible to help you track your progress. Stay on course by utilising the leapfrogging technique.

## On a Summit Plateau in Mist.

Actions.
1.   Stop.
2.   Think.
3.   Take stock of where you are.

If you are near a trig point then you will already have a good point of reference. This will help you to use an accurate bearing to plan a line of descent. Use short legs and leapfrogging to follow the planned route. If necessary also use the pace counting technique.
If you are lost then there will be a need for cautious movement. Move slowly and carefully. If there is a clear linear feature that you can follow towards safe ground then do so.
Keep well back from cliff edges and gullies if there is snow on the ground. There could be a danger from cornices. Keep an eye on the slope of the ground, if it starts to slope too steeply then be prepared to back-track up the slope.

## Lost in Pathless Terrain.

Actions.

1. Stop.
2. Think.
3. Look around you.
4. Take a re-section.

The re-section will use surrounding features in the landscape to give a rough area of position. In pathless terrain it is useful to keep repeating the re-section. If done properly it can help keep a track of your progress along the route.

## Caught Out by Nightfall.

Actions.

1. Stop.
2. At the map. How far is it to your final destination. How complex is the route.
3. If possible identify an easier route using line features and hand-rails.
4. If there is no path, use the leapfrog technique.
5. Move slowly and concentrate on the terrain.
6. Don't use the moon or stars to help follow a bearing, they do move in the night sky.

# 13. Other Problems for Navigation

We've looked at navigating in darkness and poor visibility, so what other situations can give you problems with navigation.

**1. Strong winds.**

These can make travelling on a bearing difficult. If you are not paying attention then it can be quite easy to be gently blown off-course and obviously, the further you travel then the more this problem is compounded. Also be cautious about the wind direction, never assume that it will be constant. If you're running east with the wind on your back don't gamble on the fact that if the wind is always on your back, then you'll always be heading east. Wind direction is always changing in the hills.

**2. Snow.**

Snow can cause even worse visibility conditions than darkness, for example white-out conditions in severe weather. Even when not severe it can obscure line features and handrails such as paths, tracks and even the courses of small streams. Point features like depressions and boulders can be totally hidden.

On the plus side, as long as you know where they are going, it does make following footsteps easier !

**3. Over-confidence.**

Clear weather conditions can generate an over-confidence due to the good visibility. It is easy to neglect the checking actions such as tick-off features when visibility is clear. Never be complacent, that's when mistakes are made. And always watch the talking, many a feature or control has been over-shot in the depths of a riveting conversation.

**4. Tiredness.**

Tiredness effects the thinking process, it affects judgment and makes it easier to make mistakes. The majority of navigational errors happen towards the end of a long day when concentration starts to wane. Preparation and training for long days will go some way towards conditioning the mind and body. However, as the day goes on be prepared to take longer over navigational decisions. Double check route choices. If you are in a two person event then work as a team, joint navigational decisions and tasks. Reduce the possibility of errors.

**5. Dehydration.**

One of the effects of dehydration, even mild dehydration, is muddled thinking. Obviously not something that goes well with the fine art of navigation. Plan into your course legs opportunities to stop, rest and re-hydrate. Be prepared to let this also to effect your route choice, if necessary deviate your route to obtain a source of suitable drinking water. A five or ten minute break every hour may use less time than an hours fumbling around because of a navigational error.

## 6.    Carrying an injury or equipment failure.

When your mind is occupied elsewhere through pain, discomfort or even just concern and worry about some thing that has gone wrong, then it can be very easy to make mistakes. In these situations concentration becomes key and to an extent these other distractions have to be put to the back of the mind.

# 14. Training and Exercises

As with all aspects of off-road running, regular training is essential to keep yourself sharp. You may know how to navigate but without regular practice, skills stop becoming automatic and become harder to use. With navigation the expression "use it or lose it" is very true.

The following are a selection of training exercises to help develop, improve and maintain your navigational skills. Use them, they do work.

Some of these exercises assume that you have an event partner, even if you don't use one and you navigate solo on your chosen event, a training partner can be very useful for constructive criticism and cross-fertilisation of ideas.

## Map memory
1.      Indoor exercise.
Plot a proposed route on a map, study the route for a couple of minutes and then hand the map to a partner. Describe the route to your partner who will then compare your description to the map.

2.      Outdoor exercise.
Study the map which shows the route between two controls. Put the map away and attempt to run from one control to another without reference to the map. Difficult to do but over time, the number of times that you will need to refer to the map will reduce.

## Compass work
1.      Outdoor exercise
Select a route and navigate round using only the compass to guide you. Even on a day with good visibility, ignoring all other techniques and tools and just relying on the compass will prove to be a valuable exercise.

## Controls and Attack-Point choosing
1.      Indoor exercise.
Choose a control point on a map then hand the map to a partner. Your partner has then  to choose a relevant attack point for that control. Reverse roles.

2.    Outdoor exercise.
If the exercise above, is performed with a map of your own local area,
then go out and locate the chosen attack-points and controls.

## Running on the needle
1.    Outdoor exercise.
Take a bearing to a visible feature then, without looking up towards the
feature, run as the needle directs. See how close you come to the feature.

## Pace counting
1.    Outdoor exercise
Another practical exercise is to get out onto
the open moors and leave a rucksack or
marker at your start point. Set your compass
to North, walk 100 paces on the bearing.
Stop. Set your compass to East and walk another 100 paces to that bearing. Stop Repeat
for South. Stop and repeat for West. You
should end up exactly at the point where you
started. If you haven't, practice !

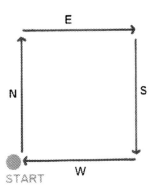

## Route choice
1.    Indoor exercise.
Sit and look at a map, choose the points to act as controls and then plot a
route between them. Select two or three possible routes and try and estimate the possible time difference between choosing each of them.

2.    Outdoor exercise
Perform the above exercise, but don't make the legs too long, and run
each route. Compare the time differences and see if you can identify why
there is a difference.

## Route choice
1.    Indoor exercise.
Look at the maps from past events, analyse your route taken and assess
whether you could have done better. Why did you chose the route you
did, could you have chosen a different route or a different attack point.
Self-criticism can be a very valuable learning tool.

## Recognising ground and terrain types

Select a route that covers a variety of ground and terrain types. Make a list of the points at which the terrain will change and what type of ground you would expect. Then run over the route and assess if what you anticipated is what you actually meet on the ground.

## Navigating in the dark and poor visibility

Don't be afraid of the dark. Go out and try to navigate a route in the darkness. Start with easy navigation and, over time, progress to harder. This will help instil confidence in your own ability. Navigating in the dark or poor visibility is a lot more scary when you've never done it before. Familiarity breeds awareness and resourcefulness.

Most people have a permanent orienteering course relatively close to them. Look up your local orienteering club on the web. This will give you details of courses and how to obtain maps. Then pop out and enjoy yourself after dark.

# Route notes.

When doing a route or race for the first time, it does help if you have basic outline planned for the route. This may save time especially in inclement weather conditions. A route card can be made from the comfort of your home prior to venturing out.

A Route note or card may look like.

Circular Route 8 miles start and finish at Crossroad GR 28592

Start.
Crossroads.
1.  Footpath to North for 1 mile.
2.  At junction take left to follow fence line.
3.  At fence/wall junction take bearing 293' to summit.
4.  Summit take bearing 48' to gate and entry to forest.
5.  Follow forest road for 2 miles.
6.  At bridge faint path bearing 23' to contour hillside.
7.  Meet footpath, turn left.
Finish
Crossroads.

Grid references may or may not be added dependant upon your own personal choice.

A route card should never be used in isolation. Always carry a map and compass, if in doubt get them out and refer.

# 15. Summary

Most runners consider navigation to be a "necessary evil", something that you need to know in order to find your way round a route. However, practice and familiarity with navigation techniques will inspire confidence in your own ability and will lead to a sense of satisfaction and enjoyment when the time comes to test those skills. It doesn't take much to reach the point where you are actively looking for the excuse to navigate.

The techniques and advice contained in this booklet will benefit those new to navigation and also those who are more experienced. It will help all those who run off-road to gain confidence in their own ability and move up a level in the navigation stakes.

Now go out and practice and above all,

## ENJOY !!

# Acknowledgements

Acknowledgements must go to Martin Bagness and his book "Mountain Navigation for Runners" which over the years both educated and inspired the pair of us ultimately leading to this publication in our series of books for off-road runners.


Also thanks to the following people for help in producing this book. Without your input, it would have been a lot harder.

Tim Barnes
Patrick Bonnet
Emma Ferguson
Gillian Ferguson
Sam Ferguson
Gerry Hehir

Steve Lumb
Mike Mallen
Harry Manuel
Rob McSherry
Lynne Shevels
Mike Tyrie

# About the Authors

Both the authors have been active outdoor people for many years and learnt their navigation skills at an early age. As solo fell runners Stu and Kev have both competed in the full spectrum of events ranging from long distance fell and mountain running, to orienteering, to mountain marathons, many of these events requiring a high degree of navigational competency.

Being qualified fell and hill running coaches, both men have, over the years, instructed and taught the fine art of navigation to fellow club members and other interested runners.

As a runner, Stu has been and still is an active competitor, even on occasion winning some races but recently he has turned his focus to devising and then going on to run new long distance rounds. These new routes include the Durham Dales Reservoir Round, the Durham Hewitt's Round and the North Pennine YHA Round. On the mountain marathon circuit his record includes:

Open Country MM 2002, 4th overall, 1st Vet team.
Lowe Alpine MM 2004, Elite course 9th overall, 1st Vet team.
Lowe Alpine MM 2005, Elite course, 12th overall, 1st Vet team.

Although a proficient navigator, due to a basic inability to run as fast as other people, Kev has never managed to achieve the same level of competitive success as Stu. But that never stopped him trying. Kev is an active member of his local search and mountain rescue team.

## The "Coaching Off-Road Running" Series

The Trailguides "Coaching Off-Road Running" series is produced in collaboration with the Run Off-Road organisation. The series is designed to promote the sport of off-road running in all its forms and to encourage participants to improve and develop their abilities and skills in order to increase their enjoyment of the sport.

Current titles in the series include:
An Introduction to Trail and Fell Running
Mountain Marathon Preparation
Long and Ultra Distance Off-Road Running
Downhill Techniques for Off-road Runners
Uphill Techniques for Off-road Runners
Navigation for Off-Road Runners

Future titles in the series will include:
Terrain Training for Off-road Runners
Strength and Conditioning for Off-road Runners
Speed Training for Off-road Runners

RUN OFF-ROAD
the organisation for promoting and
developing off-road running

---

### Disclaimer

The information contained in these pages is provided in good faith, but no warranty is made for its accuracy. The contents are, at the time of writing and to the best of my knowledge, up-to-date and correct. However, the world is a changing environment and what is correct one day may not be so the next. The suggested training regimes contained in this publication are exactly that, suggested. It is the reader's responsibility to judge their own level of fitness and whether they are capable of performing any of the said activities.

No guarantee whatsoever is provided by the author and his team and no liability is accepted for any loss, damage or injury of any kind resulting from the use of these pages. Nor as a result of any defect or inaccuracy in them.

**As with all outdoor activities, you and you alone are responsible for**